SOUTH BY SOUTHWEST

PAINTING THE CHANNEL ISLANDS

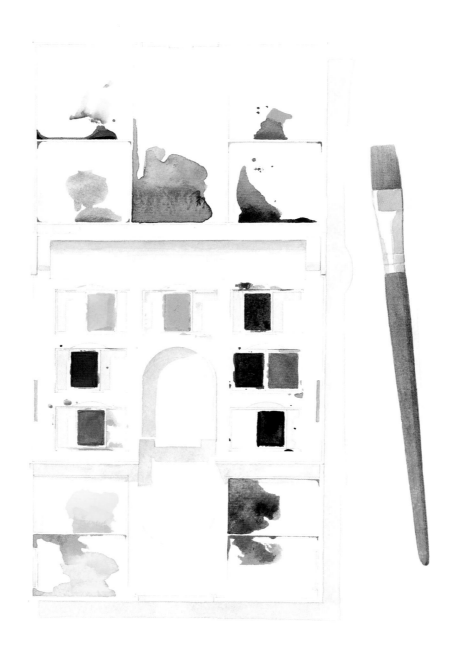

SOUTH BY SOUTHWEST

PAINTING THE CHANNEL ISLANDS

Peter Collyer

THOMAS REED PUBLICATIONS

A DIVISION OF THE ABR COMPANY LIMITED

Copyright © Thomas Reed Publications 2000

Published by
Thomas Reed Publications
(a division of The ABR Company Limited)
The Barn, Ford Farm
Bradford Leigh, Bradford on Avon
Wiltshire BA15 2RP
United Kingdom

First published in Great Britain 2000

British Library Cataloguing in Publication Data
A CIP catalogue record for this book is available from the
British Library

Edited by John Lloyd
Design and page layout by Eric Drewery
Printed in Hong Kong by Midas Printing Limited

ISBN 0 901281 84 0

Registered at Stationers' Hall

Peter Collyer is represented by
Chris Beetles Ltd, St James's, London
Telephone 020 7839 7551
Specialists in English Watercolours

CONTENTS

DEDICATION

For the Le Mas's
wherever they may be
they know who they are

ACKNOWLEDGEMENTS

I have the privilege of working with a number of people who do what they do with the utmost professionalism and are a joy to work with. If I was in the habit of wearing a hat I would take it off to them.

Chiefly I owe my success to Chris Beetles and Allan Brunton-Reed who, in their individual fields, operate with authority and panache. This work exists because of their encouragement and support.

The other three members of my team deserve special mention for their input. They are my editor John Lloyd, who magically turned my text into intelligible English; the designer of this book Eric Drewery, who is the most organised artist I have met; and Karen Willcox, who organised all my travelling by persuading most of the following to help with this project.

I am especially indebted to Jersey Harbours who supported my visits to Plateau des Minquiers and Les Écréhous. Without their help I may not have made it to either location. Peter Wilson deserves special thanks for the initial offer of help and for helping me with my ormers and bisquine. I am especially grateful to Debbie Podger who organised both of these visits and became my guide on Marmotiére.

Frank and Olive Lawrence's hospitality knows no bounds. They gave us the use of their Minquiers retreat and provided bed and breakfast in St Lawrence at either end of the visit; thank you. Thanks also to Frank and his first mate Maurice for the voyage there and back. Thanks, as well, to Roger Fauvel for making the trip to Les Écréhous in less than favourable conditions and the rest of the crew for making it so enjoyable.

I thank the following people and companies for making my visits to these lovely islands so easy and enjoyable: Richard Barneby; Buz White; Condor Ferries – Nick Dobbs and Tracey Franklin; KLM (UK) – Sue Doble; Aurigney Air Services – Ian Le Moigne; Trident Ferries – Peter Wilcox; Herm Island – Pennie and Adrian Heyworth, and, also on Herm, Mel, James and Tracy; Idlerocks Hotel – Paul Hamill; Mont de la Rocque Hotel – Diane Zachariou and John Lord; Sea View Hotel – Alan Foster; Bistro Central – Michel Thébault; Alderney Fuel Services – Rachel Sowden; Budget Cars – Sue, Jan and Simon; Captain Robert Barton and the crew of St Peter Port lifeboat; Yachting Instruments Ltd. – Bill and Ann Woodhouse; Jersey European Airways; the Duke of Richmond Hotel.

In preparing this work I pestered the following for information and I am grateful for their time and patience: Paul Aked at Jersey Meteorological Department, Johanna Burgess, Martyn Cadd, Mary Collins, Robin and Anne Dupré, Fred and Doreen Fitzhugh, Brenda Gurden, Elizabeth Hope, Alan Howell at Guernsey Museum, Philip Jeune, Roger Jones, Grant Le Marchant, Ken and Liz Le Masurier, John Lennane, Stanley and Joyce Pipet, Nathan Powell at the Met Office, Tony Rive, Martyn and Tracy Samphier, Neil Sexton at Le Tricouteur, Mike Stentiford at the Frances Le Sueur Centre and Kelly Webster.

Their help and encouragement just go to prove that no man is an island.

INTRODUCTION

At times I feel a need to apologise for being so fortunate. I enjoy my work. The rewards can differ greatly from those found in 'the real world', but they seldom seem to be related to the quality of what one produces.

A remark I often hear on returning from a painting expedition is along the lines of "did you have a good holiday?" My reply tends to be that I have not had a holiday recently. There then follows a puzzled look and "I thought you've been to . . ." "That was work." "Sure!"

You get the picture.

Some time ago I had an idea that transformed my working life. Although my paintings have not changed because of it, my subject matter has. I now write about my travels too. Under this new idea I began travelling to the far flung corners of the British Isles, even beyond, in my quest to paint the Shipping Forecast. The idea caught on and, yes, that artist being sea-sick over Newhaven lifeboat rail on BBC2 television was me.

A sell-out exhibition of the paintings *Travels Round the Shipping Forecast* at Chris Beetles' London gallery and the success of the project's book *Rain Later, Good* – three print runs so far – brought a request for more from both gallery and publisher.

In theory the world was my oyster, but I am primarily interested in the British Isles, so perhaps the world was my cockle. During my travels beyond our coasts I became aware of how different from mainland life our offshore communities are. I was captivated by one island group in particular and somewhat surprised at how unknown they were to most people on the mainland.

This is an account of my travels around the Channel Islands and if it encourages you to go there I will count it as a success.

I would like to think of this as the first of a series of books about the British islands. Having now set foot in and sat down (p152–153) in the most southerly building in the British Isles, I look forward to one day stepping inside the most northerly, Muckle Flugga lighthouse in the Shetland Islands, this time without the bucket.

On all of my Channel Island visits I was accompanied by my wife Joy. For working trips this is a bonus and a fairly unusual occurrence. But as it involved visiting the source of many a family legend as well as presenting the opportunity to meet again with long-lost cousins (and perhaps discover some previously unknown ones) it was an opportunity too good to turn down. I loved having her with me and you will meet her in the text as well as in some of my sketches.

Swanning off to Guernsey every few weeks – his view not mine – has not been the best way of persuading my son Laurie that a career in fine art can be somewhat precarious, but, as I did at his age, he is now at art college. So look out one day for Laurie Collyer's Channel Islands.

In this instance however, following in father's footsteps has meant staying at home and feeding the cats.

THE BAILIWICK OF
GUERNSEY

GUERNSEY

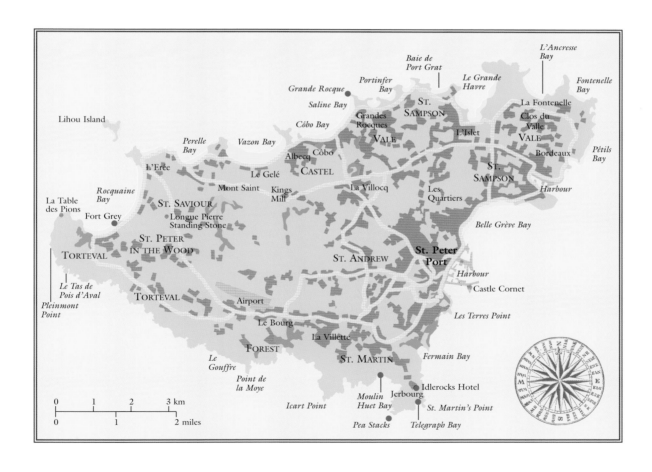

I have long wanted to get to know the Channel Islands more. The fact that they are in many ways so much like Britain and the British, yet in others so different, I find intriguing.

The first time I saw them was from several kilometres up on a flight from Heathrow to Madrid on my way to paint the weather over the Atlantic Ocean. It was about 10 am on a sunny spring morning, the air was clear and there was not a cloud to be seen. Below, the sea was a rich deep blue, the tide was out and the wide beaches glowed in the sunlight. The islands looked exotic and I wanted to go there.

On my visits for this work I did not once experience the clear, sunny crossing from, or back to Southampton that I had that spring morning. The view was always obscured by low cloud until we were approaching low over the sea on the final descent to the runway. My first and last views were always of a dark landscape set in a grey sea, more Faeroe Islands than Channel Islands. Fortunately it did not remain like that for long on any occasion.

Met Office records show, in fact, that the Channel Islands are the sunniest part of the British Isles. That, I understand, is measured in hours of sunshine. No doubt if it were measured as 'number of sunny days' it would show somewhere else like Eastbourne or Bognor Regis. That's statistics for you. If I remember one thing from my studies for A level statistics it is that you can make them show almost anything you want, but, by the generally accepted measure at the moment, it is the Channel Islands. To be more precise it is Fort Regent on

Jersey and L'Ancresse on Guernsey, but not in 1981 when it was Leuchars in Fife and Boulmer in Northumberland, but that's the weather for you.

Not wanting them to be rounded up as traitors, some nameless islanders I have spoken to are frankly somewhat suspicious of those figures, but there are other statistics to back up their perception of Channel Islands weather. There is about the same annual rainfall as Manchester, yes Manchester, more even than Edinburgh and 45% more than bracing Skegness.

In other words, like the rest of the British Isles the climate is typically maritime, but on the whole sunnier and warmer. So much more milder is it in winter that in places such as hotels, restaurants and pubs there is often a photograph of that place taken in the snow, so unusual is such an event.

For someone visiting from Britain for the first time there is something very familiar about Guernsey. In many ways you could believe that you are in Devon or Cornwall; lush pasture, wooded valleys, sandy bays sheltering between granite headlands, narrow country lanes where motorists drive on the left ... if unusually carefully and slowly.

My first impression was that there is something very civilised and 'England in the '50s' about the island, a little quaint and old fashioned and refreshingly so. For instance in the more rural areas you will notice boxes and small open fronted cabinets perched on garden walls or attached to fences and filled with garden produce for sale. They are a common sight.

Our first visit was early one March and many boxes were filled with bunches of carnations and

Jethou and Herm from the Idlerocks Hotel

bags of potatoes. From one such box I bought freesias at one fifth of the price they were in the florists back home, putting the cash into a small money box which bore the notice 'please be honest'.

If only we could turn the clock back.

An obvious difference from Britain is that many place names and nearly all of the street names are in French, giving the island a hint of an English speaking French province.

In the case of all of the Channel Islands English is the official first language, but there is a declining traditional patois, a conversational language that is a form of Norman French that William the Conqueror would have been familiar with. This varies from island to island and is different again from that spoken in Normandy. It is not the language from which modern French has evolved. That is the patois of the Paris region which was elevated to replace Royal French when the Royal French themselves were replaced.

As with modern French the occasional English word crept into common use when there was no other word available. In Guernsiais for instance a wheelbarrow would be referred to as le wheelbarrow.

The legal system is French-based and all property conveyancing is carried out in French.

Pronunciation of local place names can at times be a little unexpected, but I suppose that could be

bargain freesias

said about the whole of the British Isles. They do not always sound as French as you might expect, some have an Anglicised sound. Hanois, for instance, is pronounced Hanway and Moulin Huet Bay is called Moulin *Wet* Bay.

The Normans were Viking in origin, the Norse Men or North Men, so a number of place names have Viking endings. Ey or Oy is the Norse for an island hence Guerns-ey, Jers-ey and Aldern-ey. A small island or islet is a Holm or Hou as in Lihou, the small island off Guernsey's west coast, and Jethou and Brecqhou close to Herm and Sark.

In recent years I have travelled much around the British Isles and to the lands immediately beyond. Being in the north of Britain, Norway, the Faeroe

Islands and Iceland has given me a particular tingle of excitement and a feeling of being more where I belong. Even the briefest thought of time spent in somewhere like Reykjavik is enough to bring on a pang of separation, leading me to wonder if I have some Viking blood in me. There is a sense of that here too.

For me the island's Norse heritage appears to be more tangible than just those remnants to be found in the place names and patois. I have read many descriptions of the island's capital which compare it favourably with Mediterranean and Normandy ports and rightly so; it is picturesque. But I found in St Peter Port something very reminiscent of the north, of Lerwick in the Shetland Islands and Bergen in Norway.

Like them, the port rises steeply from the harbour over a hillside densely layered with attractive buildings, narrow cobbled streets, alleyways and long flights of steps. The collection of granite towers that punctuate the skyline and give the town such a distinctive appearance when viewed from the sea is particularly Lerwick-like, so too is the way the town has the harbour at its heart, with the main street behind the buildings on the waterfront.

St Peter Port is more green and colourful, but that is mainly due to the difference in climate, and the harbour is a mass of small craft, whereas Lerwick's is filled with deep-sea trawlers. From vantage points high up in either town overlooking the roofs of the closely packed granite buildings there are views into the harbour and out to sea, with other islands sitting offshore, Herm and Sark in the case of St Peter Port and Bressay off Lerwick. The similarity is remarkable.

As they are at opposite ends of the British Isles, with a degree of shared heritage, and have in their individual ways a political and cultural detachment from the mainland, maybe they should consider being twinned. Up Helly Aa in Guernsey, the Battle of Flowers in Shetland: wouldn't that be different?

Despite all this there is a familiarity to the centre of St Peter Port. The usual high street shops, Marks & Spencer, Next, Boots are all here. Run low on cash and seek out a cashpoint machine and the usual clearing banks are here too; Lloyds, Barclays, NatWest *et al*. Here, however, you might start to notice that things are beginning to look somewhat different. For instance, you do not stumble across a Bank of Butterfield or a Royal Bank of Canada in the average provincial high street, but you will in St Peter Port. Look more closely at the office buildings and you will be dazzled by the number of company nameplates … and you will be thankful you kept those shares in Brasso polish.

These polished plates are not just names to go with a Post Office box number. They are all substantial, fully staffed offices employing one in eight of the population.

If you are of the generation who put together the words 'rich' and 'Guernsey' and come up with that delicious extra creamy liquid that comes from those ever-so-attractive cows, think again. Things have changed. This has become the land of milk and money.

Step aside tomatoes, tourism and taxes. The main industry now is international finance, accounting for more than half of the Islands' gross domestic product.

Mr & Mrs Jonathan , Idlerocks Hotel

Somehow you expected it of Jersey, it has that sort of image, but Guernsey?

Financial services as an industry started to grow in importance in the 1960s, when horticulture and tourism were still the mainstay of the economies of both Guernsey and Jersey. Income tax had long been lower than in the UK, there was no capital gains or inheritance tax, no VAT or any other kind of purchase tax. The stability of the political system, with no parties or Prime Minister, was seen as a considerable advantage, as was the Islands' special relationship with Britain; being part of the Sterling area but independent of the political system and of the EU. Their geographical position within an hour's flight from London also contributed. It was a good place to bank and do business.

As expertise grew so the industry developed, more or less in parallel on both islands. Guernsey is a little stronger in insurance and Jersey in banking and investment and trust management. Now they have developed into respected international offshore centres competing with the likes of Hong Kong, Singapore and Luxembourg.

The statistics associated with this recently blossoming business are in the 'grains of sand on the beach' league.

Consider that Guernsey has a population of a little over 55,000. There are more than 78 banks – that is roughly one for every 700 residents – with more than £50 billion deposited. That is a staggering £1 million for every islander. There are also several hundred trust companies handling assets that could be worth over five times the value of those bank deposits. This contributes to there being more or less full employment, and local services are well provided for.

Fortunately, when you travel around Guernsey you get the impression that the island has not let this recent improvement in its fortunes go to its head. St Peter Port is still one of the most attractive small ports anywhere in Europe. There is no brash outward show of wealth in the form of sparkling towers of glass, I'm glad to say.

Considering that this is now one of the world's major financial centres life here is surprisingly easy going. Take *Filter in Turn* for instance. *Filter in Turn* is a cunning scheme to keep traffic moving at potential bottlenecks like mini-roundabouts, allowing the vehicles at the front of each queue to take it in turns to cross the junction. Can you imagine anything as polite and civilised as that working in England? How could you possibly get *Filter in Turn* rage?

Commit a traffic offence – like speeding at 26 mph – and you may find yourself being pulled over by a member of the local Constabulary. If you are a visitor from the south west of England the constable's uniform badge may have a familiar look about it. This is because there are officers from Avon and Somerset, Devon and Cornwall and other forces working in Guernsey on secondment.

To find out why, and to get a different insight into Guernsey life I spoke to the one seconded officer from my own county, Wiltshire.

Recruitment from among the island's school leavers is a problem, with the more glamorous financial services industry creaming off all the most likely candidates. The short-fall of about 15 is made up with

Vaux Bêtes – Telegraph Bay

volunteers from the mainland, bringing the number of officers to around 165. Finding recruits for this task is less of a problem; more than 50 volunteered for the one Wiltshire placement of 12 months.

Guernsey police, while pleased to be brought up to the correct number and appreciative of colleagues whose experience may be different from their own, like riot control for instance, were initially apprehensive that the mainlanders would see the task as something of a 'jolly'.

The Guernsey beat is similar to the Wiltshire one – part urban, part rural and reasonably well-healed, so a fair comparison could be made.

As I expected, my informant found Guernsey relatively quiet, but I was surprised to learn that, with so many wealthy residents, there were few burglaries. Unlike the mainland, where criminals can escape over the border into another county, offenders were generally known to the police as, being a small island, there is no escape.

Drink-related offences are higher and drugs more of a problem, at two to three times the level of the mainland. One thing he had not experienced before, except on holiday in Mediterranean countries, is the number of young people, often up to twelve hundred, found wandering the streets of St Peter Port after midnight, moving from bar to club to restaurant. Well-paid jobs in the financial services industry has given those still living at home with parents a big disposable income with which to enjoy what they see as the good life. Unfortunately he finds that in general they are even less respectful of the police than their mainland counterparts.

And Guernsey in general? It's more like the England of twenty years ago; exceptionally friendly, with a good community spirit. It has a noticeably different and better quality of life, it's a place where young women can safely walk at night.

So what of politics? I asked someone from the States to explain it to me as I found the political arrangements, and the relationship with England a little difficult to follow.

It is easy when put simply. The island is self governing, but is loyal to the Crown, therefore remains independent of the UK Parliament. There is no written agreement setting out the relationship between the Channel Islands and the UK Government.

same head. different tails

Once you start to delve into the details of how this relationship works things seem to become a little less clear. The States of Deliberation is the name of Guernsey's government. Jersey has a States Assembly. The people's elected representatives in the States are all independent, there are no political parties, and, like councillors in Britain, they are unpaid. There are 12 Conseillers, each elected for a six year term and 33 People's Deputies elected for three years. The States make the decisions that in England would be made by District, Borough and County Councils as well as Parliament. There are 10 Parishes at local level, local being a relative term here, but the Parishes each send a representative to the States for one year.

The President of the States, the Bailiff, is appointed from among the representatives by the Crown, and also serves as the Chief Magistrate. The States jurisdiction extends over the Bailiwick – Guernsey's being Alderney, Sark and Herm as well as Guernsey, although Alderney and Sark also have their own Parliaments. The Bailiwick of Jersey includes Les Écréhous and Les Minquiers, although neither of these have a permanent population.

Guernsey and Jersey, along with the Isle of Man, are Crown Dependencies. That is not to be confused with the Overseas Dependencies which are the old colonies, the remains of Empire. Both Bailiwicks have the Queen as their Head of State, a situation that came about when England became part of the Duchy of Normandy – which the Channel Islands were already part of – after the Battle of Hastings brought William, Duke of Normandy to the English throne.

When Normandy was lost to France in 1204 the Islands had the choice of staying with the English Crown or the Duchy, they chose the Crown.

The Queen appoints a Lieutenant Governor (Overseas Dependencies have a Governor General) as her representative on the island. Jersey has one too. The Lieutenant Governor can attend States Meetings. He is not allowed to vote, but can speak. In practice the Queen devolves her role to the Home Secretary in his or her role as a Privy Councillor, who then acts as an intermediary between the Lieutenant Governor and the Crown. In reality the Home Secretary gives this work on a day to day basis to his department, so thus much of the Crown's role is undertaken by the top civil servant in the Home Office.

Foreign and Defence policy are deferred to the Crown, who in turn devolves this to Parliament, including again the Home Secretary, this time as a member of the cabinet. So in effect Westminster handles these matters. For once that made sense to me.

Whenever I travel somewhere to paint where the sea and coast are going to be a primary subject, it is important that I have a room with a sea view. This enables me to decide, to ponder over breakfast, the places I will want to visit that day. Or, if the light is really special, even have a little expedition before breakfast. The weather, the sky, the state of the tide all determine the particular location or locations I will want to work that day.

Coming to Guernsey for the first time I was a little in the dark about the locations where the best views were to be enjoyed. Fortunately I had some good

Le Tas de Pois d'Amont – Pea Stacks

advice from an old friend who was a regular visitor to the island, preferring its laid back atmosphere to the brash dazzle, as he saw it, of Jersey.

A study of the Ordnance Survey map of the island will always be a reliable pointer to the best spots. The particular one I used was a 1958 edition kindly lent to me by the new minister and his wife at the local Methodist church. They were both born on Guernsey but did not meet until they went to college in, of all places, London. It hardly seems possible that moving in Methodist circles in the relatively small community on Guernsey did not bring them together before they became part of a community two hundred times bigger.

The age of the map I became reliant upon for my travels did not seem to be a problem I should be concerned about. You get the impression that in many ways things have not changed an awful lot in the intervening years.

Suitably armed with a list of the best views, the hotel was chosen. My wife, Joy has a uncanny knack (with one minor disaster) of picking out the best ones and this time was no exception, we hit the jackpot.

Do they have a sea view? This was more than merely a sea view, this was an uninterrupted panorama of the whole of the Channel Islands. Perched high on the cliff top on the east side of the Jerbourg peninsula, the Idlerocks Hotel must have the best sea view in Guernsey. That's Alderney on the horizon to the far left, Herm with Jethou just in front of it a little to the left of centre, Sark and Brecqhou a little further away and a touch to the right and, on the far right horizon in the distance,

right over there you can just make out Jersey; wow! I wouldn't mind waking up to that every morning. At night you can see the flashing of the Casquets Lighthouse to the west of Alderney down to La Corbière lighthouse on the south west tip of Jersey.

The food here was heavenly, the choice and quality both exceptional and beautifully presented. I would recommend it to anyone who wants to be pampered and treated as special, for a stay or just a meal.

The quality of food on the island generally is high, so much better than you would find if you took a similar sized area of the mainland to compare with. It is one of the joys of these islands and you would have to be anorexic not to be tempted. You could be forgiven for thinking that half the population here spend their lives preparing food and the other half eating it.

On one of my excursions I found two farmers lifting and trimming leeks. Asking if these were for markets in England or France I was surprised to learn that all 18 hectares would go to supermarkets on the island – there are only two vegetable stalls in St Peter Port market. It seemed an awful lot of leeks to be eaten by such a small population.

With the abundance of produce available at the roadside it's a surprise that anyone should need to go to a supermarket for fruit or vegetables.

In April there is a Salon Culinaire, at the end of a month long gastronomic extravaganza – go on a diet first – where local and visiting chefs rustle up a tasty snack from local produce to tempt the palate. As food illustration is a specialist art, my palette will not be tempted.

In my travels I come with a completely open mind where subject matter is concerned. I rely on a good map and my instincts. I spend as much time as I can travelling. Initially this was done by car as a tour of the island, just taking in the general appearance of the various landscapes, checking to see if the deductions I had drawn from studying the map were accurate.

I had already become familiar with Jersey before visiting Guernsey for the first time and had heard from a number of sources that the islands were very different, but I was still taken by surprise at how big that difference is.

The first thing that struck me as I began to travel around was the impression that the island is one continuous built-up area. This is not the case of course. Planning regulations, however, have allowed ribbon development to take place, so as you drive around the views of fields and open countryside are often obscured by seemingly endless lines of villas and bungalows. I knew the open country was there somewhere, I saw it as I flew in and it looks just as green as Jersey from up there.

When travelling round the coastline in particular the five year German occupation of the island is something that cannot be avoided. The difference between the Channel Islands and much of the rest of occupied Europe was the construction of the Atlantic Wall, the fortification of Europe's western seaboard from the North Cape of Norway to the Pyrenees. A tenth of all the concrete and iron that went into the construction of the Atlantic Wall was used in the Channel Islands which had enormous propaganda value. They were seen as stepping stones for the invasion of Britain and figured prominently in German post-war planning.

All round the coasts of Guernsey, Jersey and Alderney are artillery bunkers, anti-aircraft batteries, command posts and, most prominent of all, look-out towers. Even though the trenches, anti-landing

Herm & Sark panorama from The Idlerocks

which was the headquarters for the Command of the Islands, monuments to the most traumatic episode in the Islands' history.

Bookshops have shelves of occupation-related titles; reminiscences and diaries, both about those who lived through it on the islands and the many who were evacuated: 19,000 left Guernsey alone, including most men of military age, and 4,700 children, leaving behind a population of 24,000. From a British perspective, the most chilling image to be found in any of these publications must be the photograph of German soldiers marching through the streets of St Peter Port past a branch of Lloyds Bank.

obstacles, barbed wire, weapons and mines have long since been removed, the remains are prominent features of the landscape, permanent reminders that something happened here which mercifully the rest of the British Isles did not suffer.

The familiarity about Guernsey or Jersey which could lull visitors from Britain into imagining that they are still on the mainland makes the sight of one of these buildings all the more shocking. They have an inhuman, imposing, ugly presence, their architecture a stark and simple functionalism designed to express authority rather than feelings, except perhaps fear. They seem particularly prominent in Guernsey,

Such horrors were not to disturb my more detailed study of the landscape that began with a walk round the Jerbourg peninsula for a first sighting of Pea Stacks or Le Tas de Pois d'Amont. I had heard about them and had seen a reproduction of a Victorian watercolour of them, before discovering where they were exactly. This turned out to be off the southern tip of Jerbourg, only a few minutes walk round the headland from Idlerocks.

I am a sucker for stacks. I first 'found' the coastline and sea as a subject for my paintings when I was inspired by them on a visit to Ladram Bay in Devon, so they have played a significant role in the development of my career. The stacks there are free-standing pieces of cliff that have been left behind as the cliff line has retreated through erosion, forming the bay. At low tide you can safely walk out to some of them, a rare treat. They have an architectural quality, mother nature's tower blocks in rich red sandstone. My particular favourites are the chalk Old Harry Rocks at Studland in Dorset, which the Condor Ferry to St Peter Port and St Helier passes soon after leaving Poole Harbour.

Pea Stacks make a very gneiss scene. In fact the whole of the Jerbourg peninsula is made up of a variety of gneisses, including Pea Stacks gneiss, and is separated from the rest of the island, geologically speaking, by a band of quartz.

On my first visit – it was the first day of March, an overcast day of warm moist wind and poor visibility – I had intended to limit myself to a circuit of the peninsula just to familiarise myself with the landmarks and views. Rain looked imminent, but to my great surprise failed to materialise and the quality of light brought to the scene, reflected in a silvery grey/green sea, was a perfect setting for the dark and jagged appearance of the stacks; very romantic. Somehow the misty greyness had a luminous quality that seemed appropriate, a dash of sunlight would only diminish the intensity of this first encounter.

My only problem was to decide which viewpoint I should use. It was such a shame that for the purpose of my visit only one painting would be needed. I could imagine that if I lived here, it would be one of those locations that would call me back over and over again and continue to give new interest and enjoyment, a scene I would never tire of.

After spending some time clambering over the cliffs to satisfy myself that I had not missed anything more dramatic, but not wanting to venture too near the edge for fear of being blown off by the wind, I moved on round the headland.

Rabbits were everywhere. It was already quite clear to me that Guernsey is the kingdom of the rabbit. I imagine that on such a small but well populated island, where agriculture/horticulture and housing account for most of the land, undeveloped areas where they can flourish are at something of a premium. Man is its only predator, apart from cats and kestrels and the odd feral ferret that probably takes a few. There are no foxes, deer or badgers so it is, surprisingly, the largest mammal on the island, although is not a native having been introduced in the Middle Ages as a source of food.

I have spent whole days being less productive than on that brief walk from the hotel. When things are going well there is a reluctance to do anything that might break the spell, to disturb whatever it is that makes things work there. So I continued walking, for a while at least.

To the east of Pea Stacks I discovered Vaux Bêtes, Telegraph Bay. This I knew would look wonderful late morning in full sunlight, with the wind, if it continued, ruffling the water in the bay.

The day of my departure arrived before the weather was clear enough to make the clamber down the cliff worthwhile.

Telegraph Bay is even nearer to Idlerocks than Pea Stacks, within sight in fact, with the path down the cliff beginning by the corner of the hotel garden.

Moulin Huet Bay

I am making this sound too easy. Put it down to good planning.

The path leads onto a group of rocks that jut out into the sea, with a narrow concrete bridge connecting the last rock – hardly qualifying as an islet even – to the rest across a minor chasm. On a stormy day the sea crashes over this bridge and a crossing should not be attempted.

The view looking back into the bay at the cliffs more than repays the effort of the climb down – and back.

In November 1565 this was Richard Higgins' last view of Guernsey.

He was the captain of the *John* of Sandwich, that had been wrecked on the coast. The crew survived but were captured and confessed to piracy. Castle Cornet was their prison while a decision on their fate was awaited from Queen Elizabeth. She decreed that the men had been deceived into believing that their voyage was purely commercial, and as they had already been in custody some time a majority could be freed, but some should, nonetheless, be made an example of. This fate fell only to the unfortunate Richard Higgins, who was taken to the spot from which both my painting and he was executed.

It is not recorded how long he hung there before expiring, long enough to enjoy the view I hope.

He probably did not enjoy what he saw of his final day on the island quite as much as the crowd which had gathered there to witness the spectacle.

On this final rock where the gallows once stood now stands a small building with a light and a very loud fog horn to warn ships that this is St Martin's Point, the south eastern corner of Guernsey. This is also the end of the telegraph cable linking Guernsey with Jersey, so it could be said that it continues to be the spot from which messages are conveyed.

Following the coastal footpath north from St Martin's Point in good weather is a very pleasant experience indeed, taking you eventually into St Peter Port if you want to go that far. If not, at various points along the way there are paths that lead back to the St Peter Port to Jerbourg road. The footpath is

Harbour entrance with Castle Corne

very well signposted using carved pieces of pink granite at the various junctions and there is a liberal scattering of benches to rest and enjoy the views.

The path follows a natural ridge and is much nearer the sea than the cliff top, which is mostly covered, to varying degrees of density, with houses, but you are seldom aware of them. Passing round a number of small headlands and bays – one of which is Pied du Mur, or Marble Bay, where the band of quartz that crosses Jerbourg is exposed by the sea – the sounds of the sea and its bird life are joined by the sounds of the wind through the trees and birds more associated with woods and gardens. Here the cliffs are, again to varying degrees of density, wooded, making the walk feel less exposed than on many cliffs.

At various points along the walk there is a view north along the coast to Castle Cornet and, in the far distance, St Sampson. Somehow it is distance that makes Castle Cornet look even more impressive than it does from St Peter Port Harbour where it sits at the entrance. My first ever view of it was from the *Condor* ferry at night, when the castle is floodlit and looks absolutely stunning. It manages to appear at the same time both powerful and beautiful.

On this walk it was *Condor* again, this time leaving St Peter Port for St Helier, that brought it to my attention. *Condor*, gleaming in the sunlight and looking more like a space ship than a water borne one, suddenly appeared from behind the castle. I was struck by the contrast in their appearance and, from this distance at least, the similarity in their sizes and immediately thought 'a painting!'

One particular section of the footpath, marked as La Divette on maps, passes through a group of pine trees. These are much photographed and often appear on calendars and postcards. They are known as the pine forest. Having been to Scotland and Norway I have seen a pine forest or two and can only assume that this is a Guernsey example of what might be kindly referred to as rustic humour, which often manifests itself in place names.

The 14 kilometres of Guernsey's south coast from St Martin's Point to Pleinmont Point in the south western corner, is a natural fortress and makes for a very different walking experience. Steep cliffs averaging 80 metres in height are where the upland area that is the southern half of Guernsey interacts with the sea. This is cliff top walking country, exposed, often windswept, granite, gorse and gulls.

...dor arriving from Poole .. or is it Mars ?

Open country Longue Pierre Standing stone with Hanois Lighthouse in the distance

From Le Gouffre – roughly the half-way point – westward, the walk is pretty isolated, too. There are however five points at which a road or track leads off La Route de Pleinmont to the cliff top ending in small car parks, so the faint-hearted, infirm, or just those without the time, inclination or recommended protective clothing can also still enjoy the magnificent cliff scenery without making the entire trek. At Torteval the car park is next to a German bunker and just off from the base of the cliff on which it stands are more Pea Stacks. These are the minor Pea Stacks, Le Tas de Pois d'Aval.

The footpath continues round the Pleinmont headland – where there is a good view of Les Hanois lighthouse – and ends near the shoreline at a natural amphitheatre known as La Table des Pions, a spot which did once, and still could today, play a major role in Guernsey life.

This needs some explanation.

If you travel down the roads and lanes in late June or early October it is possible that you will come across some men peering up at and poking over-hanging trees and hedges. It may not look like a custom stretching back many hundreds of years, but it is. It just looks a little less ostentatious than it used to. They will be parish officials, Douzaines. This is modern Guernsey's way of maintaining each parish's responsibility for ensuring that the generally narrow roads are kept shorn of their overhangings under the States *The Cutting of Hedges Ordinance, 1953.*

In mediaeval times this was known as La Chevauchée de St Michel, a cavalcade of mounted dignitaries of the feudal court of St Michel,

accompanied by their three dozen or so pions, or footmen, and joined for part of their journey by the Lieutenant-Governor and his staff along with a regimental band. The pions were dressed in white and decorated with many red ribbons and each one carried a staff, the end of which was adorned with a red rosette. If you can imagine a mayoral procession accompanied by mounted police, a Boys' Brigade band and several sides of morris dancers you probably get the picture.

Every three years in the month of June La Chevauchée would set off, after a communal breakfast, from Vale church, St Michel du Valle, to inspect the roads to ensure that they were being properly maintained, and to ensure that the way was clear for the processions of the Blessed Sacrament. One of the officials carried a lance, 11 pre-metric feet long and if he could touch any overhanging vegetation with it the owner of the property was fined. By mid afternoon the Chevauchée reached the farthest point on their tour of inspection and sat down to a substantial *al fresco* luncheon at La Table des Pions.

After the Reformation the custom was continued with the purpose of keeping open the King's Highway.

It seems to me that La Chevauchée could be revived. The need still exists and the duty is still performed, only the manner in which it is carried out has changed. It would forge a link with Guernsey's historic past at a time when some people claim that the influx of outsiders is watering down the island's identity. It would be a spectacle with relevance both

Château de Rocquaine – Fort Grey

functionally and culturally … which is more than could be said for the Battle of Flowers.

When I discussed the cutting of hedges ordinance and my colourful revival idea I was challenged to take the opportunity to experience it at first hand.

"I'm game, as long as I'm not expected to ride a horse, wear bells on my legs or blow a bugle."

To be honest, I didn't quite know what to expect, but I somehow imagined it would involve a lot of walking and that I would be carrying the eleven foot long pole, so to be driving up and down the streets of outer St Peter Port in a smart Audi estate came as a bit of a surprise, albeit a pleasant one.

"What about all that fuchsia overhanging this wall?"

"Well it's a one way street and cars always park next to the wall and the pavement's down the other side, so I cannot see it being a problem, besides it looks so good it would be a shame to cut it back in full bloom, I think we can let that go."

"I will show you the whole patch but I only do half of it, another Douzaine covers the other half. The boundary between St Peter Port and St Martin's runs down the centre of this road, so I am responsible for this side and a St Martin's Douzaine inspects that side."

"What about all these weeds?"

"Well as they are growing out of the crack between the base of the wall and the pavement they are technically the responsibility of the States, but maybe they shouldn't be, perhaps the Ordinance should be changed to include them."

Was I here experiencing Guernsey's real battle of the flowers?

As we cruised around I was beginning to see Guernsey in an even better light than before. My first impression that the various villages have, along the roads at least, become like one semi-rural suburb needed modifying. To my surprise we were finding, even quite close to the centre of town, pieces of countryside: a field with some tethered Guernsey cows, a paddock with horses grazing, a smallholding, an old windmill converted into a jeweller's workshop and lots of trees.

Along the way we talked about the duties of a Douzaine and the various roles which you can find yourself taking on if you become involved in parish politics here. I get the impression that it involves being something of an unpaid social worker if you are willing to roll your sleeves up and get stuck in: a surgery two or three times a week, helping a poor family find shoes for a child to go to school in, or even enough food to see them through the week, and persuading the more fortunate to supply the goods or funding to make it work.

There is a States support system but in some cases it obviously is not substantial enough. It was difficult to square this with the abundant wealth of much of the island's population. In Britain this support role has been the responsibility of national government since the middle of the nineteenth century when it took over from Parish Relief, but here that old local system has been able to continue functioning successfully because the island is small enough for it to work still.

Now and again another role was described as it came to mind.

"Oh! And I'm responsible for burying any dead bodies that are washed ashore and are not claimed or cannot be identified. I have to find a coffin and arrange the funeral, and pay for them. Actually I need to find a new plot because the one we have been using is now full."

"What about the bramble poking out through that hedge?"

"She is elderly and has no-one to help her, I'll come back later with the secateurs and snip that off."

Somehow I found it difficult to imagine some of my local councillors getting that involved.

Still, I was here for painting purposes as well as to gather local colour. Moving on to the east of Le Gouffre, although still characterised by the same high cliffs, the coastline is more indented, forming a number of bays with sandy beaches and a prominent headland, Icart, from where the views are quite exceptional. Naturally, there is a car park at Icart, from where there is an easy walk round the headland to the east and a superb view across Saints and Moulin Huet Bays and the distant Pea Stacks.

Some of the beaches are more accessible than others. The best is Moulin Huet, at the end of a wooded valley which starts in a maze of narrow lanes where you can encounter the unusual art deco Captain's Hotel. The road passes the Moulin Huet pottery and steeply sloping fields where you might

Leek farmers
Torteval

Grande Rocque

see Guernsey cattle grazing. The journey ends with a flight of steps down to the beach which is in some parts sand and others rounded, sea-worn rocks.

Renoir painted here. *The* Renoir, Pierre-August Renoir, 25 February 1841 to 3 December 1919. I have to confess that I do not like his work that much, but he is about as famous as an artist can be, so I was intrigued. He stayed in Guernsey in 1883 long enough to complete 18 paintings. Apparently he was impressed with the light, a phrase often used by artists in relation to small islands, or somewhere like Cornwall which is almost entirely surrounded by sea. It is spoken of as if it is a great mystery, which I find puzzling. Surely it's simply the fact that sunlight is reflected back up off the sea onto the underside of clouds making them appear much brighter than they would have done had they been over a large land mass. Or is that too matter-of-fact an explanation?

I am not in the habit of seeking out views that other artists have painted, that seems like making life more difficult than it needs to be. I suppose that at some time I have painted a scene that another artist has gazed upon, but have been blissfully unaware of it. Yet somehow, as this was Renoir, I wanted to take a look. He painted Pea Stacks from here, but the view of them is nowhere near as impressive as the one from the headland overlooking them. From here they are *in* view rather than *the* view. It was a strange experience. What do the Guernsey artists think of this spot, I wonder? Do they frequent it or avoid it because *he* has been here?

A few years into my painting career I discovered that one of the major London galleries had packed off its stable of artists to paint the ancient track known as the Ridgeway for an exhibition. At that time this was my territory and I felt very possessive about it. I was indignant. Who did they think they were? I lived and breathed that landscape and knew all its secret little corners, all its moods in all weathers throughout the day and through all the seasons. I had in my mind a 3D virtual recreation of it and could even identify a particular spot from just a few clumps of grass. What did they know? That some of it was in Wiltshire, that empty place just off the M4 motorway? The cheek of it!

I went to see this exhibition filled with apprehension, these were some of the best contemporary landscape painters around at the time and I was sure my ego was about to be deflated. I would probably never pick up a paintbrush again. I would have been trumped in my own back yard. I'll admit the exhibition was pretty good. It should have been. There were a few thoughts of how did he do that? but I felt that I could have put my work in with theirs and it would not have looked out of place. Instead of making me feel inadequate it gave me the confidence to try for a London gallery, that very one in fact. It worked. By the time that same exhibition had been re-staged in London my work had been incorporated, I had arrived.

We're an odd lot, we painters . . .

Back in Guernsey, one day I found myself driving on La Route des Paysans in St Peter in the Wood past the Coach-house Gallery. If only we hadn't missed that turning; I'm sure Joy will readily admit, she's not the world's greatest navigator.

I did not want to be put in this situation, but I knew I had to do it. I was on their territory, the professional artists of Guernsey and could not avoid them any longer. I entered the lions den and eventually came out with a brilliant etching *West Coast* by Paul Bisson. I loved all his work. I like Paul Bisson's Guernsey.

I like mother nature's Guernsey too. What more could you ask for than the first breathtaking sight of Rocquaine Bay looking down from the heights of La Route de Pleinmont? The broad bay, framed to the north by L'Erée headland with the small island of Lihou and filled with a turquoise sea, foaming as it breaks over rocks that at low tide link Lihou with L'Erée.

For nearly a kilometre the road meanders down from the high ground to sea level, bringing you out at the southern end of Rocquaine Bay in front of the Imperial Hotel. From here the view is of the full five kilometre sweep of the bay. A granite sea wall rises about five metres from the head of the beach to form a low parapet wall at the roadside. At low tide the drop in sea level is such that the sea retreats several hundred metres, exposing an area of coarse beige/grey sand and dark blue/grey granite criss-crossed by fissures that have become filled with sand and sea water. The whole has the appearance of a beach which has for the most part been dug over, bringing to the surface a darker, partly charred material.

Belinda Jane with Fat Grey

About half a kilometre round the bay is the most striking feature of this view, and a work of man, Fort Grey.

The fort is one of many defensive towers that were built along the more vulnerable stretches of the Guernsey coast at the end of the eighteenth century, a time when an invasion from France seemed a distinct possibility. Many of the surviving towers are of a design peculiar to Guernsey and are known as loophole towers after the square holes in the walls through which muskets would have been fired.

Fort Grey is one of three Martello towers on Guernsey's west coast. They are more substantial buildings designed to carry and receive a heavier battery than the loophole towers. The fort sits on a rocky outcrop and is linked to the sea wall by a short causeway. The simplicity of its design gives the building a timeless quality. Locally it is known as 'the cup and saucer' and is now a maritime museum telling the story of the countless shipwrecks that have occurred in this area.

In the vicinity of Fort Grey I inquired if there was somewhere close by that we could get a tea or coffee and was told that there was 'a fisherman's cafe' just along the road. I had visions of a nautical version of a transport cafe, full of old sea dogs in their so'westers smelling of the wet fish counter of Sainsbury's and puffing on pipes stuffed with dried vraic. Nothing of the sort. It is a pleasant restaurant where a very nice couple put a lot of effort into dreaming up new cake recipes. They also sell a good gâche (pronounced gosh), a traditional cake-like tea loaf peculiar to Guernsey. I always enjoy a good slice of local tradition, especially when it comes spread with a generous helping of Guernsey butter.

The Fisherman's Restaurant was one of many buildings overlooking Rocquaine Bay in the localised vernacular style of single storey nineteenth century fishermen's cottages; thick granite walls often painted white, squat chimney stacks built into the gable ends, the occasional dormer window.

I had something of a déja-vu-esque experience, not exactly feeling that I had been here before, but realising that I had been somewhere else that looked remarkably like this. It was quite a shock. Suddenly I felt that I was about 885 kilometres away, as the gull flies. The sea and the granite were a common factor, geologically and geographically there were a number of similarities, but the most striking link was the buildings, they were so reminiscent of . . . the Hebrides.

Twice a day, at high tide Lihou becomes a part time Channel Island. At 7.2 hectares in area it is the smallest occupied island and with a highest point only 20.7 metres above sea level, the lowest lying. Although linked naturally by rock at low tide there is a winding causeway just under half a kilometre long which until 1994, when the island was purchased by the States of Guernsey for £435,000, only Lihou residents were allowed to use.

At the end of the causeway, looking out over Guernsey stands a 1960s granite farmhouse with a walled garden, on the site of an earlier building used for target practice during the German occupation.

On the south side of the island are traces of the early twelfth century Benedictine Priory of St Mary or Notre Dame de la Roche. Before the chapel was

built seven menhirs and three dolmen stood on the island, but no doubt to symbolise the overthrow of paganism the stones were incorporated into the foundations of the building. Although originally part of the Abbey of Mont St Michel, it now comes under the Parish of St Peter in the Wood and the Rector there has received a remuneration for his responsibility.

Lihou is barren, windswept and apart from the house, undeveloped. It is a naturally wild spot that allows us access for enough time to wander, rest and enjoy before the tide returns its isolation.

In a pocket sized version of Lihou's link with Guernsey it, too, has its own satellite, Lihoumel, the northern-most islet of a chain of rocks, the visible sign of a largely submerged reef lying across Rocquaine Bay. Many of these rocks have been given names descriptive of their appearance, cat rock – the most southerly, south of the Hanois Lighthouse – Les Aiguillons (spurs or points), La Genouinne or Nipple Rock. These rocks make for a spectacular sight on a stormy day when the sea is crashing over them and are best enjoyed from the comfort of the Fisherman's Restaurant with a slice of their coffee toffee marshmallow cake.

The displays in the Fort Grey museum illustrate the danger to ships presented by the Guernsey coastline in general and these rocks in particular.

It is said that if a Guernsey sailor died in a shipwreck it was possible to tell where on the island he came from by the design of the Guernsey sweater he wore, each parish having its own distinctive pattern. Guernsey is still synonymous with that knitted sailor's sweater, but at one time the island, along with Jersey, was famous also for knitted stockings that were the fashionable thing to wear in seventeenth century London and Paris, where they fetched four times the price of locally produced items. So lucrative was the knitwear trade in those days, it seems the whole population of the island was at it, even children and, to the alarm of the authorities, farmers who had to be threatened with imprisonment to encourage them to put away their needles and get on with the harvest.

Today only one factory in Guernsey, Le Tricouteur near L'Erée headland at Perelle Bay still makes the traditional navy blue Guernsey sweater in commercial quantities, using imported English worsted, the traditional yarn. Now they are knitted on machines, although they are still assembled by hand by a team of up to 200 outworkers, a few less than the numbers employed three hundred years ago.

The entire west coast of Guernsey from the south side of Rocquaine Bay to the east side of L'Ancresse Bay is a succession of low lying headlands, sandy bays and massive formations of pink granite, a distance of about 24 kilometres. From in front of the Imperial Hotel as far as Vale church a road hugs the coast with barely a rise or fall, only parting from the ramparts of the granite sea wall to by-pass the headlands and to change its name 21 times along the way.

Rocquaine is the largest bay. There are hotels but for the most part it is overlooked by the many low houses that sit on their long strips of land stretching away from the sea, and which in some places even appear to be below sea level. The houses are more scattered here, adding to the Hebridean flavour. At the side of the road, in gardens and in small yards, inshore fishing boats can be seen parked on trailers or standing on blocks. Rocquaine seems to have more of the traditional way of life about it.

It is easy to become bewitched by the sea and coast and to ignore the land that overlooks this corner of the island. A number of lanes climb inland from the bay onto the higher ground through countryside that is as rural and sparsely populated as Guernsey can be; meadowland, wooded valleys, picturesque cottages and farmhouses, a number of nature reserves as well as intensively farmed fields.

Beyond Perelle Bay the coast takes on more of a holiday flavour, particularly Vazon and Cobo Bays, where the broad sands are backed by many hotels and guest houses. Visiting Vazon now, you would not realise that below the sands are the remains of a forest. For centuries peat was dug out of the beach and there still exists the right to levy a toll for the nuts and acorns eaten by pigs driven into the forest, indicating that whatever caused it to disappear happened in historical times.

This coastal strip and the northern half of the island is low lying. It may not have the drama of the southern cliffs, or be as pretty as the east coast south of St Peter Port, but when travelling along the coast road there are moments of visual excitement and delight, and sights you just would not see anywhere else but Guernsey.

At times on my first visit, when everything was new and something of an adventure it was difficult keeping my eyes on the road ahead. On many occasions I found myself stopping to find somewhere to turn round in order to return to a particularly superb view. I must have annoyed many other

Guernsey cow Vale Common

motorists, perhaps there should have been a sticker in the back window, one of those orange diamonds that reads *Take care – artist on board*.

Noticing a particularly wonderful formation of pink granite, Lion Rock, as the road rounded Albecq, thinking that it could make the painting that defined the character of the west coast, I returned on a day when winds were near gale force and the weather a mixture of sunshine and heavy showers, some of them hail. Some time was spent studying the scene but I was not sure. All the elements were there and the wind was driving some spectacular waves onto the rocks, but somehow it did not click.

Moving on, I tried the next headland, Grande Rocque, and instantly I knew this was my location, it

was just a matter of exploring until I found the right spot. Clambering over the rocks near the water's edge I found the power of the waves both exhilarating and frightening. Three viewpoints were to be found that worked particularly well, but it was difficult deciding between them with it all happening in front of me. At that moment, nature was too overwhelming. Not until I was back at home in my studio, with my memories as a guide, was the choice made.

Further along the coast is a large bay, Le Grand Havre. Until 1806 the land to the north of this, Clos du Valle, was a separate island at high tide and could only be reached by ferry or a bridge on the east coast at St Sampson, two and a half kilometres away. The channel was filled in, reclaiming 120 hectares of land which was sold to fund a road building programme. Clos du Valle became a productive granite quarrying area in the mid nineteenth century and is still pockmarked with the remains of many small quarries. One has been turned into the Beaucette Marina by blasting away the cliff that separated it from the sea.

The natural harbour at St Sampson was developed to meet the demands of the granite export trade and the town has continued to grow making it Guernsey's industrial north. Whether by accident or design, one reason for St Peter Port looking so attractive is that the more unattractive aspects of life, the power station and the working harbour where you find fuel storage tanks, cranes and warehouses are conveniently out of sight at St Sampson.

Approaching Clos du Valle in the vicinity of Vale church across the former arm of the sea late one afternoon, I came across the arresting site of a number of tethered Guernsey cows being milked. Tethering was the traditional way of keeping them in order to make the most efficient use of the available pasture, but is relatively unusual now, they are more often to be found these days in large commercially efficient herds.

I have a lot of time for Guernsey cows, and Jerseys for that matter. These are cows that have got on and made something of their lives. Why have they been so successful? Is it because they look so pretty? They are small and curvaceous and seem to wear an awful lot of mascara, but would we love them quite so much if the front end looked as unappealing as the back end? They seem to carry milk and voluptuousness in equal quantities. I find them strangely alluring, if I believed in reincarnation I would like to come back as a Guernsey bull.

The real reason for their success lies in their modest appetite and the fact that they are the most economical cattle at converting their intake, making milk with a very high butter-fat content.

So how do you tell a Guernsey from a Jersey, apart from the fact that the ones you see on Guernsey are always Guernseys and those on Jersey, Jerseys? They both have inward curving horns. Guernseys are golden reddish brown with white patches, Jerseys will be a more fawn colour and are generally smaller, although both are smaller than many other breeds. Jerseys have a more rounded face with larger eyes and black noses, Guernseys have pink noses. Both breeds are rather docile. What better ambassadors for Guernsey could there possibly be than their cattle? They are just like the island itself; small, beautiful, perfectly formed, relaxed, yet productive.

ALDERNEY

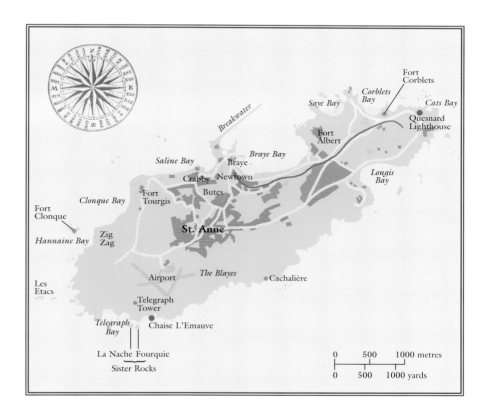

urigny is the old Norman name for Alderney which is still used today in the ceremonial parlance of the Alderney and Guernsey States and by the French. How this became corrupted over the years to Alderney is a bit of a mystery, but the name lives on with Aurigny Air Services, the only way to travel to Alderney. That does not mean that you cannot get there by any other means. In the summer ferries run from Jersey and England and a great many people get there, if not under their own steam, at least under their own sail or outboard.

My meaning is that Aurigny Air is the only way you should consider travelling, especially if you have a sense of adventure.

Aurigny is Alderney's own international airline. How many communities of only two and a half thousand people can boast that? They are proud of it and rightly so.

Alderney was the first Channel Island to have an airport, in 1935. Before that planes landed on a beach. Aurigny came into being to provide a service between Alderney and Guernsey when the previous

carrier discontinued the route. When services started in 1968 their first aircraft was the new and relatively untried Britten Norman Islander, built at Bembridge on the Isle of Wight. Flights were put on when passengers were around to fill them and the working day ended when all had been flown to their destinations. In order for final payloads to be calculated every passenger had to be weighed.

Things have progressed somewhat since then but they still provide Alderney's link with Guernsey and Jersey and a shuttle service between the two larger islands. They manage to combine the friendliness of the folks next door with the operational efficiency of a modern airline, a sort of neighbourhood Virgin Atlantic.

Most of the fleet are Britten Norman Trislanders, small 16 seaters with an engine on each wing and another on the tail-plane and a fixed undercarriage. Aurigny were the first airline to have them and still have the largest fleet with eight planes. They all have names, nothing pretentious like Spirit of St Helier or St Peter Port Clipper, nice friendly names like Jack and Joey. Joey is the star of a series of children's story books, a sort of flying Thomas the Tank Engine, and even has his/her/it's own fan club.

Production of the plane ceased in 1982 but Aurigny cannot find anything better with which to replace them. I gather from Britten Norman that following an order from China for three aircraft they have decided to recommence production hoping that more interest from there will follow. So Aurigny can now replace their fleet with some more. It looks like the Trislander will be part of the Channel Islands scene for many years to come.

In the waiting area at Guernsey Airport I counted the occupied seats. There were sixteen, a full flight. Does that mean that one lucky passenger will get to sit in the seat next to the pilot?

Joy was somewhat apprehensive about flying in such a small plane. A friend had made this journey once and described the landing as "oo-er time", recounting how they flew at the cliff face and used the updraft to flip them up onto the runway.

We drifted into conversation with a couple who had recently moved to Alderney. They detected Joy's apprehension and tried to allay her fears with an account of their last flight, just to let her know that it was all very routine.

"…We overshot the runway at the first attempt so he took it round again and put it down on the grass instead."

Well, that settled the nerves. As dusk approached it was comforting to know that if the pilot couldn't find the runway he was at least able to find a good substitute within easy walking distance of the terminal.

The flight was called and we marched out across the tarmac. Close up the Trislander looks even smaller than it does buzzing around the Islands' skies. I've seen bigger bathrooms. We stood in a loose group and while we waited to board I became aware that the force 6 which had nearly postponed our Condor crossing from Poole the previous evening was still blowing strong. I wondered how stable the Trislander was in these conditions.

We were called in fours to the plane where a metal step the size of a milk crate was placed on the ground and a door opened. Revealed inside were two pairs of

seats, not side by side with a gangway between but one pair in front of the other, just like in a car. The backs of the front seats were flipped forward to allow the passengers for the rear seats to clamber inside, just like in a two door car. Once inside, the cabin felt car-like in its width, height and leg-room, only there were eight rows of seats. You could even open the windows!

The pilot climbed in and with a "Welcome aboard this Aurigny Air Services flight to Alderney, we will be flying at one thousand feet and the journey time will be approximately twelve minutes", he started firing up the engines and we were off. He wasn't wearing a leather balaclava but somehow I felt he should be. It was strange to be able to look down the cabin and watch him actually operating the controls. There was not enough room for him to turn round and stand up to give us the tying of the straps on the life jacket routine. I tried to imagine how a hostess would pass among us dispensing refreshments. Perhaps she would crawl along the floor underneath the seats handing them up as she went. In her absence perhaps the pilot will push a straw into a Kia Ora carton and pass it back.

derelict threshing machine near the airfield

Joey landing.

Flying at a mere one thousand feet you can see every wavelet and lobster-pot buoy. I was reminded of that old joke:

Flying instructor to trainee pilot; "You'll be flying solo tomorrow."

Trainee; "How low?"

We just had to stare out of the window. All those cresting waves were mesmerising.

The Casquets lighthouse soon sailed by on the port side and Alderney's south coast began its approach from the north east. What a view!

As we turned to make our final approach with dusk drawing in as rapidly as the runway, every detail was still clearly visible below; steep granite cliffs, waves crashing against offshore rocks. I caught a brief glimpse of a ruined pier as we passed over the coastline, the ground gathering speed rapidly as it came up to meet us.

Looking down the cabin the runway lights were all that could be seen ahead, drifting to the left and then the right, then momentarily falling out of sight altogether as we lined up for a touch-down which came with a modest jolt. It was all over far too soon. What an exhilarating way to travel, we both loved every second. Imagine travelling like that all the way from Southampton.

Touching down on the island it is immediately apparent that Alderney is different.

In Jersey people will tell you that life in Guernsey is relaxed and laid back and I am inclined to agree. In Guernsey people will tell you that Alderney is relaxed and laid back. If that is the case you would expect them to be horizontal and barely conscious. While that is not strictly the situation, it is quite clear to even the most casual observer that life here is pretty easy going.

For example, on arriving at our hotel someone came out to our car to help us in with the luggage. Looking across the road he noticed his golf clubs on their trolley, parked behind his car where he had left them several hours ago having forgotten to take them in. He went on to inform me that over here people don't even bother locking their front doors.

What do the police find to do all day?

The next day I was caught by a local locking my hire car. It was pointed out to me that it must have been the only locked car on the island.

"Force of habit I'm afraid," was my reply.

I began to feel guilty. I got the impression that this single instinctive act was taken as an insult to the entire population of the island. I could see the headline in the next issue of the *Alderney Journal* VISITOR LOCKS HIS CAR – DIPLOMATIC INCIDENT SPARKED. I apologised and pleaded English in mitigation. This must have been accepted as the conversation continued.

"We always leave our keys above the sun visor."

"It saves carrying them around I suppose," I replied.

"Well, if anyone wants to use your car they know where to look without having to bother you for them."

I laughed, but he kept a straight face. It was not a joke. I think I like it here.

St Anne, where most islanders live, feels more French than anywhere else in the Channel Islands,

Sister Rocks

although the people here seem more English than on the other islands.

St Anne is compact, it doesn't spread out unnecessarily all over the countryside. Anywhere in the town is within a few minutes gentle stroll, even the airport is only fifteen minutes away on foot. A gentle stroll sums up the pace of life here, even the official guide proclaims 'a casual approach to time' evident in the opening hours of St Anne's shops. They all seem to close for an hour and a half at lunchtime; including the bakers, so if you are planning to buy a few things for a picnic don't leave it too late or even your lunch will be out to lunch.

I could not get over how trusting and friendly people are here. Take my hire car for instance, which nobody would of course. I had been using it for three days before I met anyone from the garage that supplied it – Alderney Fuel Services, next to the harbour, lovely people – and that was only because I wanted to put some petrol in it. A full tank would probably last several months here.

While I was there and as I had just seen the Police Land Rover (registration AY 999), I just happened to say in passing that I would be interested in speaking to the policeman to find out what he does all day. They asked, "which one?"

"Which one? How many do you need?"

"There's one that lives here and one they send over from Guernsey."

"I'll bet there's a stampede when that job becomes vacant. So what do two policemen find to do all day?"

"It's mostly domestic incidents. They go into the schools and talk about cycle safety, that sort of thing. We don't get the sort of trouble they do on Guernsey after the pubs close."

Even over a drink or a meal it's surprising where a conversation takes you. I cannot remember how Milk-a-punch Sunday came up, but I do remember that it is peculiar to Alderney.

We were paying a second visit to the lovely Georgian House Hotel in the centre of town. Perhaps assuming that most folk have a blow-out lunchtime, on a Sunday evening they do a splendid high class buffet instead of the usual menu. I recommend it highly. The proprietor told us about the first Sunday in May, when it used to be permissible to milk anyone's cow in the field and take eggs from under anyone's hen. On that day, to celebrate the cows going out to grass, every licenced premises offers its regulars a glass of milk-a-punch.

Here is a recipe: To suggest that this is *the* recipe would be foolish, everyone has their own with its secret ingredient. Of course all are the best.

Whisk 5 eggs with 140 g of caster sugar. Stir in 2·75 litres (5 pints) of fresh milk and flavour with freshly grated nutmeg. Add one bottle of rum, all of it, which should be stirred slowly into the milk to prevent curdling. The magic ingredient could be a tot of brandy. This is supposed to be the correct amount for ten to twelve people. If you are a solitary soul it might be wise to reduce the quantities a little, just in case it is several days before you are found.

The Georgian House is a little more grand than many of its neighbours in the centre of St Anne. Most are built in rows or at least close together,

The Georgian House
St Anne

lining narrow cobbled streets on a hilly site that slopes generally down to the north meeting the sea at Braye Bay, where the harbour is. The undulating setting adds to the town's attractiveness. None of the streets are particularly straight, so you never see too far as the road disappears enticingly up or down and round the next bend.

At two points several streets meet forming squares of differing character. Royal Connaught Square is the more enclosed and is framed by several fine buildings, the grandest of which is the eighteenth century Island Hall. In its time this has been the Government House, an hotel and a convent. During the German occupation it was the Soldatenheim, the German equivalent of the NAAFI, and now it is home to the library, the monthly People's Meetings (where the electorate discuss items on the States agenda) and the annual Christmas pantomime. In the centre of the square is an Indian Chestnut tree from Windsor Great Park, planted by the Queen when she was still Princess Elizabeth.

At the centre of the other, more open Marais Square is a huge cattle trough. The name Marais suggests that this was once a marshy area and cattle were traditionally brought here from the Blayes, the nearby communal agricultural land, to drink. The present trough was provided in the 1880s.

Filling one wall in the dining area of the Marais Hotel that overlooks the square is a splendid Edwardian photograph, greatly enlarged and full of life and detail, of a cattle auction in the square. Packed with people of all ages and prime examples of the now extinct Alderney cow, it is a wonderful piece of social history and for a first-time visitor like me, a reminder that before tourism, offshore banking and disc-zone parking, St Anne functioned as a small market town like hundreds of others the length and breadth of the British Isles.

From Marais Square, taking Little Street through the southern fringe of St Anne you climb up to the Blayes which occupies part of the plateau that makes up the western half of the island. From the end of the narrow tarmac road an unmade track leads out onto this still largely agricultural area, the most open and isolated spot I have found in the whole of these islands. The peace is broken only by the sound of the wind and the occasional Trislander. This was the only area of level ground large enough for the airport. Visiting at a quiet period in the agricultural calendar and out of the main tourist season I had this largely to myself.

It really is a surprisingly lonely spot. The main airport buildings lie hidden in a slight dip on the north side of the airfield between the runway and St Anne and you can walk west from here along the cliff top footpath or, a little further inland, along the unmade track and see only one building in two or three hours, depending on how often you stop to admire the views.

When the path reaches the cliff top you are standing on the southern edge of the island at its broadest point, but still only two and a half kilometres away from Fort Tourgis on the north coast. From here, visibility permitting, it is possible to make out the other Channel Islands between the south and southwest points of the compass.

Looking across to the east and more likely to be visible as it is a mere 15 kilometres away from this spot is the coast of France. Just beyond the northernmost point, Cap de la Hague, stands the Cap lighthouse and way down the coast to the south it is usually possible to make out the giant golf-ball-like structures of Dielette nuclear power station. At the nearest point, however, the prominent collection of hill top buildings is the site of Beaumont-Hague nuclear reprocessing plant, France's equivalent of Sellafield. It's interesting that of all the possible locations the one chosen was that closest to a part of the British Isles. Pure coincidence, I'm sure. It's nice to know that a century on, the entente cordiale is still functioning as well as ever.

In the front section of the Bailiwick of Guernsey telephone directory there are two pages on what to do in the event of a nuclear accident occurring. You don't get that with BT.

Just along the Alderney coast from here are the remains of Cachalière Pier that I spotted from the Trislander as we came into land. The pier was built to enable granite to be taken away by sea from nearby quarries. It was partly destroyed by the German occupying forces because they thought it would be

Sister Rocks and pinnacles, Telegraph Bay

Quesnard Lighthouse

used by the British when they invaded! The clockwise circular walk from here takes you past some of the most spectacular coastal scenery to be seen anywhere in the Channel Islands. The cliffs here are about 75 metres high and covered in heather and bracken. You have to pick your way through this carefully in places as the path is not as well worn as the quality of the views suggest it should be.

The first awe-inspiring sight you encounter is that of two large offshore rocks known as Sister Rocks, or individually as La Nache and Fourquie. They are seen across a rocky bay from a promontory known as Chaise L'Emauve or more commonly the Lover's Chair.

There are a number of local legends about various unlikely or mismatched lovers associated with this spot. In these one or both fall accidentally or leap purposefully into space from here; alone, hand in hand or entwined. Quite why it's a chair not a sofa, or even more appropriate to their assignations, a bed, we are not told. Whatever the reason, it was thoughtful of mother nature to provide a seat, albeit very close to the edge, from which to enjoy a truly breathtaking view, and somewhere out of the wind to attempt a painting. Thank you.

Further along the path, over the headland by which the sisters lurk, you find yourself overlooking Telegraph Bay with, at the left hand end, a view of the sisters from the other side. As a view of the sisters I would say that this is the lesser of the two, as from this angle the larger one obscures the view of the other. However, scattered around this bay are a number of slightly smaller stacks and pinnacles

making this, too, a pretty stupendous sight. I was tipped off before my visit that this was a special place and it certainly lived up to its billing.

It is apparently a favourite if somewhat inaccessible swimming spot for locals. There are caves, rock pools and, at low tide, a sandy beach. All 250 of the steps down from the cliff top, however, were fenced off as being dangerous. I would think the only means of access now would be by boat or to abseil down from the top.

This used to be known as Fouleur Bay. The telegraph came along at the end of the eighteenth century in the form of a semaphore signalling station linking Alderney with Jersey and Guernsey via Sark, to be replaced sixty years later by a cable from Guernsey that went on to Weymouth. The old telegraph tower about 200 metres back from the cliff, and now a house, is the only building along this walk.

This is a spot I would want to return to again, but next time to experience it from down on the water. Sightseeing boat trips are available at times from the harbour so I can see that I will have to return to Alderney at a time nearer to the main holiday season to fulfil this wish.

In my work I try as much as possible to paint views that are accessible to anyone, I am not seeking out the most inaccessible or deeply obscure locations. I usually find my way around using the means available to all. I rarely have access to any special equipment or forms of transport that get me to views that no one else can enjoy, for me that would be pointless. I want you to be able to enjoy this view too. That is partly what my work is all about, drawing attention to these wonderful locations. If I can get here to enjoy this walk then so can you, so lace on those walking boots and get out here immediately.

Having said that, oh, to be able to fly! Just round the corner from Telegraph Bay is yet another spectacle. I am running out of superlatives for this stretch of coastline already. Here there is a rare sight from somewhere so populated and accessible; a gannet colony on Les Etacs, or Garden Rocks as they are more commonly known. Gannets usually inhabit only remote rocks and an expedition would normally be required to get this good a view, so bring your binoculars as these rocks are no more than 400 metres offshore.

The rocks are white because gannets do what all seabirds seem to do best, and as two to three thousand are estimated to live here you can imagine how much guano accumulates. I understand that winter storms can wash it all off and in spring it starts piling up again. Perhaps they are not rocks at all, it may be just a sandbank under all that.

In the more westerly distance, a little to the right of the Casquets, but not so far out, a neighbouring gannet colony can be seen. This white rock is Ortac.

May I here offer a word of warning? The cliffs here do not come to a sudden end and then drop sheer into the sea. If only they did. They curve away gently, inviting you to go just that extra step further to get a better view as you peer down into the water below. This would not be so risky if, like much of the coastline here, it was reliably firm, solid, crumble free granite, but it is not. Here the granite is capped with a layer of gravelly sand and when dry there is nothing for a shoe to grip, it is all very loose under foot.

The headland here bears the remains of some very substantial German gun emplacements and is a warren of underground passages and bunkers. On the whole, although just as plentiful as on Guernsey or Jersey, the remains of the German occupation are less visible here; which is a surprise as the effect in human terms was more dramatic. Unlike the other islands, Alderney's entire population was evacuated just before the invasion and returned to find their island in ruins. Close to the telegraph tower was Lager Sylt, the only concentration camp on British soil. The entrance pillars to the site, together with two concrete sentry boxes still remain as gruesome sentinels.

When looking at the rest of the island, however, you are overwhelmed by the fortifications, but these are British and Victorian, designed to keep out the French. The island is a mere five and a half kilometres long with a coastline of about 18 kilometres and along most of the south and west coasts, a natural fortress, there are none. Along the remaining 60% of the coast, which is low lying, there are twelve. These are not isolated towers or mere abandoned foundations poking through undergrowth, they are substantial sites with massive curtain walls; artillery positions, barrack blocks, an arsenal.

From the sea, if you catch a Condor ferry from Poole that takes the route to the east of Ortac and therefore close to Alderney, you can see these defences to their best effect. The island looks like one massive garrison. By the time they were finished,

however, artillery technology had moved on so far they were more or less obsolete.

This could have been a visual disaster. They had the potential to destroy the natural beauty of their sites, and close up some of them are somewhat overpowering, but that was their job after all. Where Alderney was fortunate was in having an architect who appears to have had a vivid imagination and a sense of romance.

In Alderney's splendid isolation, away from the gaze of superiors he must have let his imagination get the better of him, producing a collection of buildings which are more reminiscent of a period several hundred years earlier, even down to the arrow slits.

Fort Clonque

The use of locally quarried stone for these coastal fortifications, sited for the most part on areas where the rock is already exposed gives them a perfect natural camouflage. From the sea attention is drawn to the larger ones, particularly Fort Grosnez and Fort Albert guarding the harbour entrance, because of the unnaturally straight lines of their curtain walls, but the smaller offshore forts blend into the background beautifully.

From the landward side Fort Clonque off the west coast is particularly picturesque, with its round towers and drawbridge it appears to grow naturally out of the islet on which it perches. And what a name! I could imagine it on Trumpton. Access to the fort is across a causeway but one of the best views is from high up on the cliffs, allowing a view into it. There is a footpath which winds its way gently down the cliff to the causeway that is known as Zig Zag. A less well defined track branches off this path near its beginning and takes you a little to the south, through more blackberry bushes than I have seen in my life before, into a secluded valley between two headlands, from where the first sight of the fort is breathtaking.

This had to be a painting.

If you share my romanticism, take heart; Fort Clonque belongs to the Landmark Trust and is available to hire as a holiday home.

The eastern half of the island is quite different in character from the western. It is undulating but generally low lying, with a rocky shoreline and many offshore reefs and islets. This side of the island has been extensively quarried, but the abandoned workings are not particularly obtrusive.

On the north coast, between its defences but hardly hidden from view, is the famous or infamous breakwater, sheltering Braye harbour. There is quite a saga attached to the breakwater which continues to this day. Planned as an integral part of the fort construction scheme in 1847, it was to be one of two, enclosing enough water to shelter the British Fleet. The second was never started. It was deemed to be complete at nearly 1,500 metres after seventeen years, during which time parts of it had been swept away by storms, thousands of men had been employed and a million and a quarter pounds spent, five times the cost of building the forts.

Fort Corblets and the lighthouse, Corblets Bay

Eventually it was shortened to its present length. The high cost of maintaining it, now the responsibility of Guernsey as their contribution to the British defence budget, is a bone of contention between the Guernsey authorities, who think it too costly, and the Alderney people who cannot manage without it. It protects the commercial harbour, provides shelter for many visiting yachts and safeguards Braye Beach, the best on the island.

The road out from the centre of St Anne is more or less down hill all the way to the beach at Corblets Bay at the far end of the island. On the way you pass a house on the edge of the town with a blue commem-orative plaque indicating that this had been the home of the late John Arlott, wine connoisseur and for many years the voice of cricket commentary on BBC radio. Somewhere at this end of the island is also the house of former England cricketer Ian Botham. Your secret is safe Ian, no one wants to say which one it is.

The road passes Alderney Golf Course, then crosses Longis Common, where cattle graze and yet more blackberry bushes rampage out of control. I think Alderney's residents must have a collective allergy to blackberries. Why aren't they out there picking them? They're gorgeous. There must be something in this that could be used to attract

autumn visitors. Maybe they could be made into a blackberry version of Crème de Cassis, with people coming over from England and France to tread them in the vats and get to understand each other's culture better in the process; a sort of entente cordial.

I can see the attraction of living here for those of independent means who just want to get away from it all, but still have company and be in civilised surroundings. Unlike the other main islands there is no restriction on house purchases. If you can afford it you can have it. There seems to be a problem however with property and businesses owned by non-residents. There are far too many holiday homes that lie empty for many months, no longer available to residents. These also force up prices beyond the reach of young, potentially productive locals. The greater part of the profits do not get spent on the island, they disappear into bank accounts elsewhere.

Unlike the south western corner of the island there are a number of isolated houses to be found here – and some that are well hidden and not so easily found – enjoying the sea views. One building stands out from the rest, and it should. It's the lighthouse. At night the rotating beam of light can be seen from Braye Bay sweeping across the sky, even though the building is hidden from view. I gather, although have not seen it, that the beam illuminates the top of the spire of St Anne's Parish Church, which must be a little spooky.

I knew as soon as I saw it that it would become the subject of a painting, the problem is that lighthouses tend to dominate somewhat if you are too close. The question was, should I go for a wander and find something nearby to put into the foreground as a distraction, or just stay close and let it disappear off the top of the painting?

SARK

Wherever you travel around the British Isles you inevitably find places that have a familiar look or feel to them, bringing to mind somewhere else. I have experienced it a number of times here in the Channel Islands, with reminders of places as far apart as Lundy and Lerwick, but I can quite safely claim that there is nowhere else remotely like Sark.

The island is a natural fortress, protected by towering cliffs that create a sense of isolation. It is this apparent isolation which has given Sark its fame, as if the outside world is unable to scale those cliffs.

Most people will know it as the place without motor cars. Some will point out that it is the only place in the western world still governed by a feudal system. While these statements are both true, they can give a false impression of the reality.

Pictures of horse drawn carriages are a familiar part of Sark's publicity. The carriages are used to carry visitors about on sight seeing tours of the island

and they share the eleven or so kilometres of road with many bicycles. Most people seem to get around on foot, sharing the road with the carriages and cycles as there are no pavements. The roads are unmetalled, with a surface of granite chippings and earth.

The gentle rattle of the carriage wheels and the occasional ring of a cycle bell are a blessed relief from the drone of traffic on the other three large islands. This quiet unhurried scene is a precious glimpse back into a rural Britain before the arrival of the internal combustion engine and the metalled grey strip which bears it, with its jarring yellow and white markings and ghastly clutter of signs. When looking along one of these fume-free Sark roads, where the surface takes on the natural hue of the landscape through which it travels, blending into its surroundings so perfectly, a lump comes to one's throat to see the beauty of what we have destroyed everywhere else.

But wait, what's that familiar noise I hear shattering the tranquillity? It sounds like . . . yes, it is, a tractor. Not surprising really, as between them the 560 residents have about 60 of them. Well, if that is all the law here allows it's the next best thing to a car, van, truck or bus, I suppose. Somehow they manage to fulfil all of those roles, but do they really need 60 of them on an island only five by two and a half kilometres? I suspect not. Perhaps if some could be restricted to solely field use, and a number owned collectively, nationalised for communal use, they might find that they need fewer.

Car free? Yes. Motorised traffic free? Certainly not, but the life expectancy of the average Sark hedgehog is probably much longer than on the mainland.

Sark is the smallest independent state in the British Commonwealth and its system of government has its roots in feudalism. Sark was granted to its first Seigneur, or Lord of the Manor, a Jersey man named Helier de Carteret in 1565 by Queen Elizabeth I, on condition that within two years it should be populated with at least 40 men.

He divided the island into 40 tènements of varying size, each with its own coastal strip, a condition of the tenancy being that each section of coastline be defended. With each tènement came a seat in the Chief Pleas, the island's parliament. The tènements have been handed down through the generations to the present day (unless sold) by the principle of primogeniture, that is, the first born son inherits all. This has ensured that the 40 tènements have remained unchanged, otherwise by now each would have been sub-divided so many times they would be postage stamp size and next to useless.

The present owners of these properties still have seats in the Chief Pleas, the entitlement coming with the land. It is hardly democratic, but those with a land stake at least can take some responsibility for their island way of life.

Today the Chief Pleas is augmented by twelve peoples' deputies elected by the population of the island. That works out roughly to one member for every 47 people, not a bad ratio, although they themselves are outnumbered more than three to one by the tenants. In such a small community, where everyone's lives are so closely interconnected, it would be hard to imagine decisions being taken which the rest of the population would find repugnant.

Point Robert Lighthouse

The islanders are happy with this system. They see that it has served them well for more than four hundred years and they would like to keep things as they are. However, they find themselves in a struggle to continue this way of life with an outside world intolerant of a system which it sees as being ageist and sexist.

They now feel pressured into making unwanted changes which they hope will be seen as sufficient, before an outside body like the European Court of Human Rights steps in and inflicts something more dramatic on them. They want to make as few changes as possible, so have set about making themselves Strasbourg-proof.

Ten constitutional workshops were established, allowing the population of the island to discuss openly the laws which they felt needed changing and how to change them in a way that would be acceptable to themselves and, in particular, the European Court of Human Rights.

Primogenitor has been changed. Still only one person can inherit a tènement in order to keep them intact, but it can now be willed to any child male or female, not necessarily the first born. This change brings its own problems. Everyone knew the old system and accepted that when property was handed down a generation the younger children would miss out. The owner now has the unenviable task of choosing between his or her children, having to explain to those overlooked why, or to sell up and divide the proceeds. How long will it be, I wonder, before pressure builds to change the law again enabling all to have an equal share?

Reform of the Chief Pleas will half the number of tenants eligible to vote there. Those who can vote will themselves have to be elected from amongst the forty tenants, thus democracy will be brought to the previously unelected element of the parliament.

Travel to Sark has to be by boat. Aircraft are only allowed to land in an emergency, or if carrying a visiting VIP. Even over-flying at less than 600 metres is not permitted, in case the tranquillity is broken. This is a touch ironic, I think, as the current Seigneur is a former aircraft design engineer.

There are two harbours on the east coast, joined at the base of Harbour Hill like Siamese twins. Maseline, the northerly one is used for freight and by the ferries from Guernsey, Jersey and France. To the south, beyond a small headland is the older Creux Harbour, reputedly one of the smallest in the world, which dries at low tide. This is used by local boats and visiting yachts, and the boat that brings day visitors across from nearby Herm. To reach Harbour Hill from either harbour you pass through tunnels, blasted through a rock wall.

Sark is an undulating plateau generally 75 to 90 metres above sea level and the harbours are the only coastal development. To reach the rest of the island you need to negotiate Harbour Hill, a road which winds itself up the cliff face through a wooded valley. It's very attractive, and a good footpath takes a slightly different and more direct route to the top. Unless you are young, a glutton for punishment, or fitter than nature intended, I wouldn't recommend it. Save walking for the journey down.

There is an alternative and after all, it's not every day you get the opportunity to ride in a toast-rack; at least, that is what the locals call them. A Sark toast-rack is a tractor drawn bus. There are two of them to meet visiting boats. Bench seats are arranged back to back across the trailers, so with only a small stretch of the imagination they do look vaguely like toast racks on wheels. We paid our fare and climbed aboard, dainty farmhouse wholemeals sitting next to crusty grande rustiques and powered up the hill. If speed is your thing, make the most of it because at the top you'll find that things start to … slow … down; wonderful!

Tractors are not allowed to carry passengers around the island, only up and down Harbour Hill. They also have a curfew imposed upon them, having to be off the roads by 10 pm. At the top you disembark and that's when you get the full impact of Sark's difference. And what a difference! It must be said that Sark is not backward, it just has not needed to develop as far, or at least in the same way, as anywhere else.

This is the village, thought by some not to rank among the island's many beauties, but it is in this 'built up' area, a relative term here, that the

approaching Maseline harbour

Sark from the west, early morning

differences stand out. One can argue that as far as most people are concerned a cliff is a cliff and a field is a field wherever you are, but it is when we start building that a place's individual character is most striking. Here it strikes so hard it knocks you over in amazement.

Everything is on a human scale. Buildings and roads are small and trees look big, like they should. Life is carried on at a gentle pace. Horse drawn carriages line up to ferry visitors off on voyages of discovery through space and time. The joy of walking on a surface free from the geometry of paving slabs and tarmac is indescribable. We strolled about aimlessly at first, just taking in the wonder of it all, eventually opting for a walk along The Avenue.

At some time in the past, as the name suggests, this Avenue was a tree-lined driveway which led to the original seigneurie. Today it is a shop-lined road with a gallery, cafe, gift shop, food store and the Post Office among them. They are an odd collection of buildings, mostly single storey, traditional, modern, some attractive and some not so, some with only a semi-permanent look about them. This is downtown Sark, but the concentration of buildings only lasts for a hundred metres or so before it all begins to change to a more open and attractive scene, isolated buildings set back from the road, with gardens and plenty of trees.

At the far end of The Avenue you will find one of the island's schools. It was a surprise to learn that such a small population manages to support three schools, with one for five to seven year olds, one for juniors from seven to nine and one for seniors up to sixteen. Seniors sit an eleven plus type of exam and if they pass the authorities will pay for them to go off the island. The pupil to teacher ratio is an enviable eleven to one, but there are only about 35 children in total. Sark, in fact, pioneered modern free education, making it obligatory in 1827, more than fifty years ahead of the mainland. The first school was for boys only.

Against the school wall leaned a line of cycles several deep. Contemplating these over lunch in a neighbouring tea-shop garden I decided that the way to get to all corners of the island in the time we had at our disposal was to hire a cycle. It cost just a few pounds.

As I prepared to clamber aboard it suddenly came to me that I had not ridden one of these contraptions for more than fifteen years, and never one with a wicker basket on the front. Oh dear, was I about to make a fool of myself? My bag containing my sketching paraphernalia fitted neatly into the basket, so at least I would not have that swinging loose around my neck, pulling me one way when I needed to lean the other.

Off I went, a trifle wobbly at first, but soon it all comes back. The granite chippings make for a bumpy ride but there is no point trying to swerve round them, you just peddle like mad and hang on, exercising muscles again that must have thought they had taken early retirement.

Oh dear, there's a bend coming up with a pot hole. I think I'm going too fast and I haven't quite mastered cornering yet. That handy basket obscures the view of the front wheel and when I turn the

The Avenue

handlebars the blasted thing still points straight ahead. Better make sure the bell works … Sorry madam … no it's only a scratch, I'll be alright. I'll just lie here for a while and watch the clouds.

The island seems so much more hilly from the saddle, but on the whole getting about is much quicker. I would highly recommend it and I am sure that vibration therapy cures something you didn't know you had.

The roads are fairly straight and follow courses unchanged in four hundred years. In the vicinity of the village they are laid out in a typically mediaeval grid pattern. Away from the village many are lined with earth banks, the most common type of field boundary, no doubt designed to give some protection against the wind. Hedges grow along many of the banks, but there are groups of fields where trees are something of a scarcity. These tend to grow mainly in sheltered valleys near the coast.

A neat rectangular pattern of fields stretches across the entire island, in many places right to the cliff tops, but there are a few areas of bracken, gorse and blackberry covered common, where the cliff edge is less well defined and no doubt the soil is poorer.

Cycling along these lanes untroubled by passing vehicles was a real treat. It was so peaceful and the air so fresh. It was strange to see roads so empty. I could not help noticing that almost every field had an old bathtub in it; no doubt for the Guernsey cattle to drink out of rather than perform their ablutions in. Occasionally I would come across a Sarkee who always had a smile and a welcoming "good after-

noon" as I clattered past. I felt as if I had all the time in the world to stop occasionally and soak up the sweet atmosphere.

This leisurely time I imagined as I cycled along belies the hard work that goes with everyday life on the island. Many jobs are seasonal, especially those dependent on visitors. Most fishermen are in the shellfish trade, which has a closed season. Their boats are laid up out of the water for the winter to prevent them from being damaged in storms. Many people have more than one job, fishing perhaps in the summer and building maintenance or re-decorating one of the hotels in the winter.

Even the boat builder is part time. I found his yard, not where you would expect the boat builder to work, but down a track near a cliff top along the north-east coast, about two and a half kilometres from the harbour.

The size of a Sark-built boat is restricted by the bore of the tunnels blasted through the rocks for access, as the harbour is the only place they can be launched. The boat is craned onto a trailer at the yard and pulled down the narrow roads to the harbour, where it is craned into the water. This has to be done early in the morning before the carriages start work as it frightens the horses.

Quite a celebration takes place when a new boat is launched, with food and drink, a blessing from the parish priest and the customary bottle of champagne broken on the prow.

Whether from a boat or from the cliffs themselves, all of the island's coastline is pretty stunning. All round the coast the cliffs are penetrated by many

Banquette Bay

the old mill & mine bike

caves and at Port du Moulin and La Grande Moie there are impressive natural arches.

Having to arrive by boat means that you get a seal's eye view of some of it anyway and for some that might be enough. Sight seeing boat trips are advertised in a number of the shop windows in The Avenue and if the weather is good it will be a trip to remember. The west coast is particularly dramatic and the one visitors are likely to miss, of course, as the harbours are on the east side of the island.

Because of the way the island's tènements were originally created there is little public access to considerable sections of the coastline. There is no coastal footpath encircling Sark like there is on the other Channel Islands, but there are quite a few places, the commons, where footpaths lead off the road to the cliffs, with most of these having short walkable sections of path along the cliff tops.

I cycled to the four corners of the island. You can do that here as it is roughly diamond shaped. There is an exceptionally fine view looking south along the west coast from Eperquerie Common at the far north just where the road ends. Here there are a number of footpaths across the common and the occasional seat where you can recover from the ride and take in the wonderful view. This I had to paint.

Rue de Moulin, a continuation of The Avenue leads out towards the west coast at the island's widest point. The tower of a sail-less windmill is passed along the way as is a substantial duck pond with a

pretty cottage. At a turn in the road a track, easy to miss, passes between a cottage and a farm entrance and out past a field of grazing sheep, through a field gate and onto the bracken covered Gouliot Headland.

In the distance you can see Guernsey, Herm and Jethou. On the headland immediately to the south stands an obelisk above 299 steps leading down to a landing, used only when an easterly gale prevents a safe entry to the east coast harbours. Looking north there is a good view along the coast towards Eperquerie Common. The most dramatic view, how-ever, is right in front of you. Off the headland sits the granite fortress of Brecqhou and this is the best view you are likely to get of it.

Back towards the mill is a crossroads. From here the road south takes you to Little Sark, joined to the rest of Sark for the moment, but one day it could become as detached, geographically, as Brecqhou.

Between Sark and Little Sark is La Coupée, probably Sark's most spectacular and most photo-graphed natural feature. It is a narrow causeway not much more than a cart's width, 100 metres long, with a drop of 80 metres into the sea on either side. This had to be negotiated without the aid of a handrail before 1900. On windy days Little Sark children going to school would have to crawl across. It has now been strengthened and the road across becomes a firm strip of concrete, but cyclists still have to dismount.

The bays on either side, which are separated by La Coupée, are protected by headlands, no doubt preventing the full force of the sea eroding it away. Somehow I get the impression that if man had been foolish enough to have constructed something as delicate as this across this gap, everyone would have said at the time "I'll give one good storm and that will be the end of that".

Even mother nature is defiantly different here.

From La Coupée there is the only major length of cliff top footpath, taking you back eventually to the village. It is not the most direct route, but if you have the time the scenery is pretty special here, too. The view from the path that leads to the Derrible Headland is the best and as you approach the end of the path here, too, you will find yourself staring down over an 80 metres cliff edge into the sea.

Cycling along the roads, noticing people going about their everyday business helped me to come to

looking south from the top of Harbour Hill

Joy with wintering fishing boats, Creux harbour

terms with the island. When I arrived on Sark I did not know quite what to make of it, being so very different from anywhere I had experienced before. Once I became used to it, then came the uneasy feeling that we, as visitors, shouldn't be here. It felt like we were prying into someone's private life. But the income made from tourism helps them to sustain their way of life, and if you come just to enjoy the peace and quiet and the warmth of the people then maybe that is alright.

Sark is certainly unique, but I cannot help thinking that this is how life should be and somehow everyone else has got it all horribly wrong. I tried to imagine living here myself. Would I find it too claustrophobic?

I spoke to an islander who moved here from the mainland many years ago. She finds it claustrophobic at times. She explained that when there have been a few damp and grey winter days she just feels the need to escape.

Lots of people buy from catalogues and belong to book or video clubs. Sometimes, but less often nowadays, bad weather will prevent a supply boat from sailing. You may go to the butchers and find a sign 'No Boat No Meat'. A delay in the delivery of newspapers seems to cause the most consternation.

I asked if I could live here, to which she replied, "sure, if you can afford it". There may not be any income tax or VAT, but house prices are high and nearly everything has to be imported, with two lots of transport costs to add into prices; one to Guernsey from the mainland and one from Guernsey to Sark. People are assessed for tax on their visible wealth, so it pays to be bohemian and that usual status symbol the motor car is no use as a guide.

Mentally you would have to be fairly self contained and like your own company, while at the same time being a social sort of person throwing yourself into all the aspects of island life.

It's quite obvious that Sark is a close-knit community. People look out for each other. There is no system of welfare so they would need to, but you get the impression that everyone is so close they would do it anyway.

There are two books which are good for getting a flavour of real Sark. Ken Howard's *Sark*, which is particularly good on the history of the island and Jennifer Cochrane's excellent *Life on Sark*, an account of day to day life taken in monthly bites, starting in April. From the latter the strong

field with bath

community spirit shines through. The number of events is quite extraordinary and at times bizarre.

For instance, there is a water carnival where one of the events is for man-powered flying machines to attempt an aerial crossing of Creux harbour. On new year's day they do really silly things, like holding an Oxford and Cambridge boat race through the streets on wheeled carts (they do not have a river), but still propelling themselves along with oars. On another new year's day a group of men scaled the north face of the Bel Air Inn, horizontally along the road, roped together like real climbers. The film of this event, made at a 90 degrees angle to give the impression of a real climb, is apparently quite convincing until a dog runs in front of the camera.

I think the time I would like to be here is at Christmas. They seem to have retained some semblance of sanity long lost everywhere else.

That would be my testament for the island generally. No matter what the outside world might think of their system of government and the way of life defined by it, I would go for this any day.

There must be something seriously wrong with our thinking if we deem that Sark has got it wrong and we have got it right.

BRECQHOU

north side from the Herm–Sark boat

Information about anything connected with Brecqhou is, to say the least, a little variable. Even its size is up for grabs: I have read in one book that it is 40 hectares and in another 65 hectares. One thing that does not seem to be in doubt, however, is the fact that since 1993 Brecqhou has been owned by two brothers. They are reputed to have paid £2.33m or £3.5m for it; take your pick. You see the trouble I had researching this?

I have looked up a number of newspaper articles about their ownership of the island and their relationship with Sark. In these they are often referred to as being reclusive, so I will refrain from mentioning their names here. You know what they say about things you read in newspapers and they should know, they own one or two, or at least one of them does ... apparently.

Certainly if you want to be a recluse Brecqhou is

ideal. Sark itself is thought by many to be somewhat off the beaten track, if you could have such a thing across open sea, so living on a rock 75 metres off Sark should keep you well out of the way.

Brecqhou sits off Sark's west coast, sloping away from it like a giant wedge of Shropshire Blue cheese. About two thirds of the way down the island, nestling in a natural depression near the north coast and out of sight from most of Sark's nearby cliff tops the brothers have built themselves a new house. A house is hardly the right description. This is more a gothic castle complete with towers, turrets and castellated battlements. The architect was Quinlan Terry, Britain's most noted copyist of historical styles, whose previous work includes the much praised Riverside Development in Richmond and the Cathedral of SS Mary and Helen in Brentwood.

Alderney, Guernsey and Jersey have more than their fair share of fortifications so another one will probably not go amiss. It's good to see someone keeping up the tradition. This hardly looks like the house of someone who wants to keep a low profile, though, as you can see it from Guernsey.

One of the brothers has also drawn attention to their position by writing about it in the national press, criticising Sark's system of government and letting everyone know just how much it has cost them so far (£1.75m) attempting to change it. They might have started by taking the strength of their argument to the Chief Pleas, but the seat there which they inherited with the island has never been taken up. If you are not a great fan of the feudal way of life,

and Sark is the only place left in the western world that has it, maybe this is not the most ideal place to move to.

Brecqhou is approximately a kilometre in length from east to west and about one third of that from north to south, with a headland projecting from the south coast. A 65 metres cliff faces towards Sark and the island tapers to low cliffs at the western point with a six metres high rock, Moie Batard, bearing a navigation mark joined to it at low tide.

Geologically the island is an extension of Sark and like its close neighbour has many caves. A local legend claims they are home to rats, descended from some which left a sinking ship carrying passengers escaping the bubonic plague in London. That's just the sort of story which might be spread by smugglers wanting to store their contraband somewhere out of sight.

The island is not known for its long history of habitation. There is no ruined monastery, ancient derelict sheep enclosure, prehistoric dolmen or menhir. King Arthur is not thought to be buried there, Leifur Eriksson is not known to have used it as a staging post on his voyage to discover America, even St Brendan the Navigator does not claim to have rowed ashore in his coracle to celebrate mass with the puffins.

For most of man's occupation of the Islands Brecqhou seems to have been nothing more than a good place to graze livestock or to go rabbiting. Occupation of the island did not begin until the second quarter of the nineteenth century when a farmhouse was built. On and off for most of the next

North side of Brecqhou from Sark

Brecqhou from Gouliot Headland on Sark

hundred years a handful of people lived there, growing cereals and vegetables and grazing sheep.

In 1929 Dame Sibyl Hathaway, the then Seigneur of Sark sold Brecqhou to a former Guernsey hotelier for £3,000. Along with ownership of the island came for the first time a seat on Sark's Chief Pleas, this right being transferred from one of her tènements by Dame Sibyl. After only three years the island had a new owner who made many changes, including the building of a grand house, improvements to the water supply, the installation of an electricity generator and the construction of an aerial cableway to transport supplies and cattle.

The house stood unoccupied but still furnished during the German occupation of the Channel Islands, changing hands again in 1947 or 1949, depending on the source, when it was bought by a reclusive Scottish textile baron and, according to some sources, his brother for £15,000. They/he stayed for eighteen years before selling to a millionaire industrialist and merchant banker who managed to knock down the £120,000 or £125,000 asking price to a more modest £44,000 or £46,000. Somehow he managed to persuade the Chief Pleas that what they wanted in order to preserve the peace and quiet of the two islands was the sound of his helicopter ferrying him to and from his business meetings. During his stay ponies and donkeys were raised and more building work undertaken.

It was six years after his death before the present owners moved in with their helicopter.

During construction of their 'castle' rumours about the building and what might be included in the plans began to circulate locally. The project architects found it necessary to take out a full page advertisement in the *Guernsey Press*, in the days when the paper was still a broadsheet, to point out that it was a private development, that there were no plans for a casino or nuclear fallout or atomic shelter and that there was no security service vetting for employees or contractors.

The newspaper printed long lens photographs of the building under construction and as a result ran into some legal difficulties. Eventually a reporter was allowed ashore to write an article which was illustrated with authorised photographs, but the negatives had to be surrendered once they had been used.

The 1930s house was eventually demolished, after providing accommodation for some of those working on the new one. The new building is faced with granite imported from Spain. There are still a number of working granite quarries in the Channel Islands but these supply mainly chippings for road construction. The quarrying methods and stone dressing skills sadly are no longer available for a job like this.

I asked for permission to go ashore to paint on the island, dealing through an office in Monte Carlo. After two months, during which time I was told they had obtained a copy of my last book, permission was refused. Consequently I have painted the island from viewpoints found on Sark and from the Herm to Sark boat.

The views of Sark's dramatic west coast from Brecqhou must be stunning. We shall never know.

BRECQHOU

Brecqhou seen across Grande Grève
from Little Sark

I may be a painter of reality, but I can dream.

The romantic isolation of Brecqhou appeals to one side of my nature, although the reality of the solitary existence does not. If the view of Sark from there has half the drama of the view of Brecqhou from Sark's Gouliot Headland I want it. So, if you are reading this in the book shop please buy it and make a contribution to my purchase fund. I'll then be ready when the brothers sell up.

The first change I would make would be to construct a cable car across the Gouliot Passage, so that I can go to Sark to commune with my neighbours and they can come to me.

I would then demolish all the buildings on the island; turning back the clock and taking my home-building cue from Brecqhou's first inhabitants, the rabbits. At the highest point of the island I would build a house in a hole in the ground, top lit by natural light from inconspicuous ground hugging glass blisters, one of which would be a viewing platform/studio from which I could paint Sark. The natural materials would become an integral part of the building's design and decoration, rather like the Frank Lloyd Wright house *Falling Water*, although in this case it's more likely to be running water.

Oh dear, that's reality starting to creep back into the dream . . .

HERM

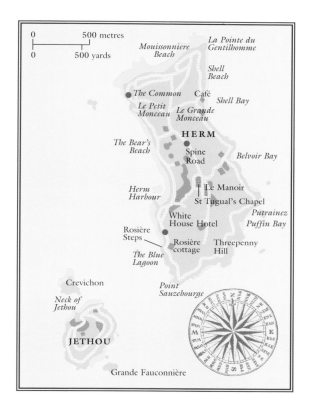

My paternal grandmother's maiden name was Lovell. I have not yet discovered the link between her and the Apollo astronaut James Lovell, but I am sure there is one. Like him I have blasted off from Earth bound for a place in a sea of tranquillity; unlike him I landed.

Space travel has moved on since he made his trips, now it is so much easier. For instance I did not have to wear one of those bulky metallic suits with vacuum cleaner hoses sticking out of it. I went in my everyday clothes. Although the flight aboard the spacecraft *Trident* lasted 105 earth years, on board it was over in only twenty minutes. Instead of having a tiny porthole with the blackness of space beyond to peer at, I experience a virtual-reality 3D re-creation of a ferry journey from St Peter Port to help pass the time. So real was this sensation that at times I felt as if I was actually walking around the boat, breathing in natural air, smelling a warm sea breeze and hearing every subtle sound in glorious surround-sound stereo as I watched the harbour slip away behind us. What an experience!

When I opened the airlock and stepped outside to take my small step for man, it was just like stepping ashore from that imaginary ferry onto an old granite quayside, only now the surroundings were real, but just as fantastic. A turquoise sea, palm trees swaying in the warm breeze, other-worldly yet strangely familiar, silent and peaceful.

Where was this extraordinary place? Why did it look so much like earth? Was this a glimpse into an idyllic past or a perfect future? It surely could not be the accessible present, could it?

Reaching into my pocket I pulled out a map which I had picked up at the start of my voyage. Maybe this had the answer.

Herm. Part of this world but light years away.

Rugged cliffs in the south and sandy beaches in the north, a hilly centre with wooded valleys leading down to the shore, a northern common of undulating grassland. An island idyll, and only 700 by 2400 metres, about 200 hectares. This small island appears like a vision from a dream and to a certain extent it is. Its great beauty is not wholly a process of nature.

Major Peter and Jenny Wood with their two children came here in 1949 from England, having obtained the long term lease of the island from the States of Guernsey, which had purchased the island from the Crown in 1947. Neglected and overgrown buildings stood derelict and there was no power or water supply or drainage. Granite had been quarried and the abandoned workings left their scars on the landscape. It took them three weeks even to find their house.

They had a vision of how wonderful Herm could be and began the long process of recovering its natural charms, as well as embarking on a programme of sympathetic development that would allow the island to provide them with a living. All this had to be carried out while making the island available for visitors to enjoy, a condition of their tenancy.

Jenny Wood told the story of how they eventually realised their dream in a wonderful book *Herm Our Island Home*, which is still available on the island. It is an essential read for anyone who ever had a thought of escaping from mainland life as most of us experience it, or for those bent on just doing something beyond the ordinary.

Sadly the Major and his wife are no longer here to enjoy the fruits of their labours. The lease however has been extended to 2049 and transferred to a company, Wood of Herm Ltd, which is owned entirely by members of the family, thus ensuring that future generations will continue the management of the island. Pennie, the Major and Jenny's daughter, the first of their children to be born on Herm, and her husband Adrian Heyworth run the island today with the same dedication and energy. We must all be grateful to them for keeping to that original vision, so that we, too, can come here to this gentle spot and dream.

It is just the perfect place.

What makes the island magical is what isn't here, most notably the motor car and everything that comes with it, like roads, parking areas and pollution.

Guernsey cattle

There are a couple of tractors and those small four wheeled motorcycles with balloon-like off-road tyres, but apart from these the island is blissfully traffic free.

What is here, however, is exceptional. Close to the harbour there is a wonderfully comfortable and friendly country house hotel, a restaurant, a pub and a cafe, together with a shop and a post office in a Mediterranean style piazza, built by Italians who came specifically for that task. On the opposite side of the island are two kiosk cafes. All are of the highest quality, beautifully managed with great care and attention to every detail, as they so truthfully say in the guide books.

The island's strength lies in the perfect balance between the provision of visitor facilities and the careful management of the landscape which keeps it looking natural.

Herm is so peaceful and relaxing it makes St Peter Port look like Manhattan. Most visitors making the trip over from Guernsey on the Trident ferry are here for a day, to spend the time relaxing on a quiet beach, or to take a gentle stroll along the coastal footpath. The island is small enough for most people to be able to manage a complete circuit in half a day at a fairly leisurely pace. Those arriving for a stay at the White House Hotel, or in one of the self-catering cottages, are met at the quayside and have their luggage whisked away on a tractor so on arrival it is waiting in their rooms for them; how very civilised.

The most taxing decisions you will have to make seem to be; how do I want my oysters? which flavour Herm dairy ice cream shall I have this time? or, shall I walk clockwise or anticlockwise round the island?

The latter is the most difficult. I noticed on my first day that most visitors seemed to favour the clockwise route. This takes you north along two thirds of the west coast, across the top of the island to the east coast and then on to a point about a third of the way down it. You arrive at the first refreshment stop at Shell Bay cafe without having been more than 10 metres above sea level. A good number seem not to stray far from this spot before returning to catch the last ferry back to Guernsey, and who will criticise them for that?

From there the path rises gently to its highest point of about 50 metres, along the south coast, and then back round to the west coast where the descent to hotel level is down a series of steps.

I chose to go anticlockwise. Negotiating the steps, either up or down, seemed more sensible with fresh legs, once at the top it is then, more or less, down hill all the way.

We were a party of three; me with my wife Joy and Geoff, an old school friend who has accompanied me on many painting excursions and has also joined us on several family holidays. He is more widely travelled than we, but, like us, enjoys most exploring new places closer to home. This was to be uncharted territory for all of us and it was not long before he was likening it to somewhere he is familiar with, the Greek islands. Good weather helps to create a favourable impression of course, after only a few hundred metres we were so hot we had stripped down to our shirt sleeves and this was the first week in October.

We had as our guide the excellent map of the island published by the Woods. It has the look of the

north coast beach

old OS Pathfinder series, that's the one with every building and field boundary marked, but in this case has the imperial scale of a whopping twelve inches to the mile.

Navigating your way around the island is greatly aided by a series of signposts which not only indicate the direction of the various bays, beaches and landmarks but also, uniquely in my experience, the time it takes to walk there. What a wonderful idea, but probably one that would only work satisfactorily on somewhere as small as Herm as the various locations are so close together. We found from our own experience that these timings assume you are going straight there, the problem is that everything here is so beautiful you keep stopping to take it all in.

Going south from the harbour the footpath passes in front of the hotel before rising gently, passing an overgrown quarry, reaching after a short distance Rosière Steps. Fortunately for the landscape quarrying did not become a hugely profitable business, but nevertheless the scars are visible here and there and at Rosière it is quite clear that some of the hillside has been removed. It serves a useful purpose, however, being the place where the island's rubbish is burnt. It's little details like the disposal of rubbish that tend to get overlooked when one goes misty eyed about island life.

Herm granite was used in London, so if you find yourself there and want to escape from the hectic rush, take yourself off to the Duke of York Steps in

looking inland at Point Sanzebourge

West coast from the Common

Waterloo Place, between Pall Mall and Carlton House Terrace, close your eyes and dream of Herm and you will be magically transported there. Well, at least you'll be standing on some slabs of it.

On the hillside to the south of the quarry stands the white painted Rosière cottage, overlooking a small bay which on the map is marked as The Blue Lagoon. On this day at least there seemed to be no exaggeration, the sea all round the island was an exotic deep turquoise/blue.

At Rosière there is another harbour, albeit a small one. At three hours either side of low tide the water at the main quay near the hotel is too shallow for the ferry, or any boat for that matter, to dock, so Rosière becomes Herm's terminal two. A series of wide concrete steps disappear into the water and there is a handrail to steady you as you embark or disembark. We arrived in time to see the approach of the Trident ferry at the end of its short journey from St Peter Port on one of the day's seven round trips.

At the top of the steps a stone archway with a castellated top creates a welcoming entrance to the island. It dates from the end of the nineteenth century, when Herm was the home of Prince Gebhard Lebrecht Blücher von Wahlstatt III, a member of the Prussian aristocracy. During his 25 year 'reign' he carried out many improvements to the island's buildings and planted the Monterey pines which are a distinctive feature of the landscape. He also imported animals including emus and wallabies to create a game reserve.

A series of steps take the footpath from near the archway up the side of the cliff to a height of about 35 metres. From here, with some rising and falling the path follows a meandering cliff top course round the southern side of the island, at times with an almost sheer drop on the seaward side. From this section of path the views across to the near neighbouring islands are particularly fine.

The first to come into view is Jethou, which can be seen from almost anywhere on Herm's west coast, but on this first section of the footpath, where the views west are uninterrupted, it can only be about 700 metres away.

At Herm's southwestern tip, Point Sauzebourge, the path turns a corner and starts to head north eastish. As you follow the path round the Point, Sark with Brecqhou and, conditions permitting, Jersey suddenly come into view. On this occasion Jersey appeared no more than a faint blue silhouette sitting on the horizon, but it was recognisable by the rock standing clear of its south western corner on which the Corbière lighthouse stands. Much nearer, the rugged sunlit headlands and shaded bays of Sark's west coast stood out crisply across seven kilometres of sea.

Herm is a Channel Island where you are always aware of being on an island. It is surrounded by the others and whichever way you look out to sea there is always one of the neighbours in view.

Standing at Point Sauzebourge to take in this magnificent panorama it is easy to miss what is happening on Herm itself at this point. Step forward off the path and turn around and you will see a beautiful natural corner of the island; a huge expanse of lichen-spotted granite, domed, smooth and fissured, with glorious gorse and, behind, a hillside

Trident ferry arriving at Rosière Steps

covered in bracken. For much of its history, before the island became populated and cleared for agriculture most of Herm would have looked like this. It offers quite a contrast to the prepared grassy meadowland we see as we pass round the edge of the field called Fairy Rings, when the path reaches the island's south eastern corner only a short distance away.

It is worth making the journey to Herm just to stand at this spot and enjoy the full 360 degree view.

The view of Sark remains until you turn the corner at the point farthest from here, La Pointe du Gentilhomme at the north eastern corner of Herm.

From Point Sauzebourge the footpath rises and falls, including some more steps, and it is from here onwards that the coastline of Herm itself becomes the magnificent star attraction. The headlands and bays and offshore rocks make it a particularly enjoyable walk with "oohs!" and "ahs!" at every turn. The view south from the northern side of Puffin Bay, with the grass covered rock, Putrainez in the foreground and Sark sitting on the horizon is especially good.

The name implies that puffins live in this area. They do, but only in late spring and early summer. Understandably all these islands make something of the presence of these pied charmers with their rainbow beaks.

Before too long Belvoir Bay is reached. Unlike the Vale of Belvoir in Leicestershire or Belvoir Park in Belfast, both of which are pronounced beaver, this is pronounced bel–vwar, as you might expect with the coastline of Normandy being visible in the east.

It is at this point that one has to engage the brain again, for choices must be made. Firstly there is a cafe, with that wonderful ice cream. Then there is the bay itself. The beach is inviting, with the sight and sound of the sea. Do we stay or carry on for another eleven minutes until we reach the next beach and cafe? And, oh dear, even more decisions are called for. The path at this point divides and one branch disappears into a beautiful wooded valley taking you up to the centre of the island. If you take this path, at the top of the hill it joins Spine Road. A slightly misleading name as it is not a road at all but a fairly substantial track, but it does run roughly north– south along the spine of the upland part of the island, so in that at least the name has meaning.

As that Spine Road junction is only a minute's walk away from where we were staying we decided to continue along the coastal path, to what for many visitors is the highlight of their visit to Herm, Shell Beach. As the name suggests this is a beach made almost entirely of shells, but that hardly begins to describe the magnificent sight that greets you there.

The beach, in Herm terms, is huge, about 800 metres in length, wide at high tide and wider at low. The shells are mostly fragments, but below and along the high tide mark, usually indicated naturally with a line of seaweed deposits, there are a great many complete shells, mostly very small and of the prettiest colours, shells you just will not find anywhere else in the British Isles. The magic of this shell collection is that it is deposited here by the Gulf Stream and they come from as far away as Mexico and the Caribbean.

When the beach is populated you will notice that there are almost as many people walking along with heads down shell hunting as there are swimming or sun-bathing. Come out of season like we did and you will have it all to yourself.

We were now in the low-lying northern third of the island, the Common, made up mostly of sand deposits held together with grasses and bracken, surrounded by a number of beaches each with its own distinctive outlook and character. The common looks as though it could be made into a nine hole golf course with very little modification needed. Fortunately this is something the Heyworths would never consider, although during the tenancy of Lord Perry of Stock Harvard in the 1920s and 1930s that is exactly what it was.

In Neolithic times, about 3500 to 4000 years ago, this area of Herm was a burial ground and

hunting — Shell Beach

there are a number of dolmens, or burial chambers, to be seen, particularly in the area of Roberts Cross, where Spine Road joins the Common, and around the nearby hill, Le Petit Monceau. A number of people who have come to know Herm well through living here for many years have described finding the atmosphere around these sites particularly disturbing.

Prince Blücher's farm bailiff occasionally heard a terrifying roar. On one early January morning while he was trapping rabbits, a willow tree under which he was standing bowed over to the ground and there was "an

Puffin Bay, with Putrainez and a distant Sark

HERM

indescribable noise which seemed to rush past him like a wind" which apparently left him quivering with fright.

Sir Compton Mackenzie, who became the tenant of Herm after the prince, also describes experiencing "deep authentic panic" and suddenly becoming aware of "elemental spirits all around" him.

Jenny Wood also describes this area of the Common as being "strangely disquieting".

I couldn't write that without a shiver running down my spine. Perhaps the name of Spine Road has been shortened from Shivers-Down-the-Spine Road.

101

'Moss' field off Spine Road   — Alderney in the distance

Spine Road climbs gently up from Roberts Cross between Le Petit Monceau which overlooks The Bear's Beach on the west coast and across to St Sampson in Guernsey and Le Grand Monceau which overlooks Shell Bay. The track is lined on both sides with granite boulders marking field boundaries and on the west side one field is also bounded with an attractive line of Monterey pines. The fields either side are often populated with Guernsey cattle.

At the top of the hill, where the ground begins to level out there stands a substantial group of buildings at the heart of the island, Le Manoir. These were originally a collection of granite farm buildings roughly grouped in a square around a courtyard and from a distance they look like a mediaeval fortified manor or a small castle.

Facing Spine Road stands a row of restored Victorian terraced cottages and between them and the road is a large barn housing the diesel generators that supply the island's electricity. Behind these are a collection of barns and outbuildings which have been converted into self-catering holiday apartments and cottages. We stayed here and enjoyed both their luxury and great views.

The island has about 50 permanent staff, many of them with young families, so one of these buildings is also the island's primary school, with a full time teacher employed by Guernsey States. The island manages without a doctor, a policeman, or a fireman. All these roles have to be shared among the more senior members of staff, who have received special training for their auxiliary positions in the community.

From a distance you notice that rising above the buildings, castle-like, is a castellated tower. The square 'keep' was added by Prince Blücher and close by is a taller, slimmer tower that was once a mill. Next to the towers stand two substantial houses; Le Manoir, also castellated, which was created by the prince and Lady Perry's House which is now home to the Heyworths.

This is also the site of Herm's oldest building, the small St Tugual's Chapel. Quite who St Tugual was is not known for certain. One theory is that he was the son of a king of Brittany, another that she was a Welsh woman killed by Saxons. The building is Norman and L-shaped, with a vaulted ceiling and some excellent stained glass added by the Woods family, who hold non-denominational services here every Sunday morning. We were bowled over by the fragrance of the fresh freesias and roses placed on each window sill.

Spine Road passes to the east side of Le Manoir and meets with the lane from Belvoir before continuing south to the cliff top path mid-way along the southern cliffs at Threepenny Hill. A lane branches off immediately to the north of Le Manoir, passing round the terraced cottages and holiday apartments and past the walled garden in front of the Manor, which has St Tugual's Chapel in one corner. This lane is known as The Drive and after passing the buildings it begins to wind its way steeply down a pretty wooded hillside, joining with the west coast paths next to the harbour between the hotel and the post office, at a point known to the residents as Piccadilly Circus.

When all the visitors have returned to St Peter Port on the last ferry of the day, the island is left to the residents and those staying at the White House, in the apartments and cottages, or one of the two campsites overlooking the east coast.

There is a lovely friendly atmosphere, a good spirit about the place. It is as if we all know that, whoever we might be, we share each other's special delight in having discovered this wonderful island.

Eating on Herm is a real treat. The Mermaid Restaurant and the White House both serve Herm oysters, fresh from the oyster beds which can be seen just to the north of the harbour at low tide. Knowing that they are about a sixth of the price they would be on the mainland makes them seem all the more tasty.

There is a special atmosphere at the White House. There are no television sets or telephones in the rooms and after dinner everyone retires to the lounges where they sit around in comfortable armchairs, sipping coffee and chatting, reading or playing board games. The evening drifts on endlessly if you let it.

The age of most of the hotel's residents contrasts sharply with that of its employees. One evening we spent some time chatting to an elderly lady who befriended us on our first afternoon. She seemed very knowledgeable about the island and everyone associated with it and, noticing her St Peter Port shops bags, we somehow assumed that she was a resident herself.

"Oh no, I just come here for my holiday." "How long for?" "About a month. This is my second time this year. I've been coming here for about eight years."

We also got the impression that she was from the south of England, Surrey or Sussex, but no, we were wrong there too.

"I live in Madeira." "Madeira?"

Somehow that seemed like a pretty good recommendation for Herm. If it has the power to lure someone away from Madeira for two months a year it must be special.

heaven [hevən] *n.* place or state of supreme bliss.

paradise [pærədais] *n.* place or condition that fulfils all one's desires or aspirations.

Herm [herm] *n.* place of supreme bliss where all one's desires or aspirations are fulfilled.

Herm sweet Herm.

JETHOU

Jethou with Fauconnière from Herm

Jethou is a hill with a house on it, surrounded by water.

I have simplified matters somewhat.

Jethou is an oval dome covering about 18 hectares, rising steeply at first then levelling out to a small plateau at a height of 68 metres. At one time it was joined to its close neighbour Herm, but they were separated from one another in a great storm in 700AD. At the end of the nineteenth century a four metre thick raised beach was discovered at four metres above sea level, indicating that the island was once smaller than it appears today. Included with the island are two small islets; Crevichon just to the north and Grande Fauconnière to the south which is joined to Jethou at low tide.

On the north side of the island stands a painted granite manor house and two bungalows with assorted boathouses, a jetty and a slipway.

Jethou was the first of the Channel Islands to become the possession of the English Crown, when the others were part of the Duchy of Normandy. For much of the Middle Ages it belonged to the Abbey of Mont St Michel. Robert Duke of Normandy had given Jethou to his ship-master who, after becoming a monk, bequeathed the island to the Abbey.

Although it is thought that no one lived on Jethou for most of this period it gave the Abbey an income from the sea wreck rights that came with its possession, the waters around it being notoriously difficult. In the seventeenth century the island became a game reserve for the Governors of Guernsey when it is said to have been populated by rabbits, pheasants and even fallow deer.

Since 1715 a succession of private individuals have leased Jethou, first from the Crown but more recently sub-let through the States of Guernsey. In the eighteenth century, if stories are to be believed, the motivation for some tenants was the smuggling opportunities the island offered and in the nineteenth century the potential profits to be made from the quarrying of granite. Crevichon seems to have suffered particularly from this practice, with a large section removed from its northern slope, especially noticeable from the south west coast of Herm.

Probably the island's most well-known tenant was the author Sir Compton Mackenzie, who lived here from 1923 to 1930. Originally he held the tenancy of Herm and Jethou together, but found their joint upkeep beyond his means, selling the lease of Herm to Lord Perry, the Ford Motor Company's UK agent. Lord Perry tried also to buy the lease for Jethou, where he intended to grow plants for the chemicals industry, but this was resisted by Sir Compton. In 1958, on learning that the island was on the market again he wrote, 'Jethou is the most perfect small island off the coast of the British Isles'; a pretty good endorsement from someone who was a noted islandphile.

In the recent past there has been a period of public access, with a cafe and, before that, a tavern on the island to serve visitors, and there was always the right of Guernsey residents to go there to gather vraic. Today the island is occupied by its twenty fifth tenants and remains private with no landing permitted.

Good views of Jethou, weather permitting, are to be had from the ferries that sail from St Peter Port to Sark which pass just to the south of the island and those to Herm which pass to the north. A Trident ferry arriving at low tide, which has to use the more southerly Rosière Steps landing on Herm gives as close a view of Jethou as any mere member of the public is likely to get.

My closest encounter with the island came on March 4th 1999, the RNLI's 175th anniversary day. My previous book *Rain Later, Good* in which I painted my way around the sea areas and coastal stations of the BBC's Shipping Forecast had been adopted by the charity as their 175th anniversary publication.

Asked if I would like to go out aboard a lifeboat on the anniversary day I indicated that I would love to join in their celebrations, but would be in Guernsey on my first working visit for *South by*

Jethou with Grande Fauconnière and Crevichon

Southwest. No problem, you can go out on the St Peter Port boat came the reply. Thinking this would involve a short trip along the coast, maybe to St Sampson and back, I was delighted that we eventually managed an exhilarating hour and a half at near full throttle in a force 4 to 5, completing a circuit of Sark.

On our way out, and no doubt to impress the reporters from the local radio, television and newspaper we had on board, we passed through the narrow, shallow and rocky Neck of Jethou, between Jethou and Crevichon. Show offs! Do not attempt this with your own boat.

My studies of the island were made from the south west coast of Herm, where the views of it are from a more elevated position. It appears in the distance in the painting looking out from the Idlerocks Hotel on Guernsey and in the background of the painting of Herm's west coast from the Common. The quarrying-reduced islet of Crevichon is in the background of the sketch of the Trident ferry arriving at Rosière Steps, Herm.

Looking back westward from the Barbara's Leap headland on the southern coast of Herm, Jethou aligns perfectly with the distant Jerbourg peninsular on Guernsey, even the angle of the cliff's slope matches. Were these once part of the same line of cliffs I wonder?

Searching for information about somewhere as small as Jethou can prove a little difficult. In this case there are sometimes a couple of pages in a history book which might have more than two hundred on Guernsey, or there may be a paragraph or two in a guide book, which might throw up an odd little fact as if to suggest it's small and secluded so it must be a little strange. Here is one I found:

'. . . the tenant is forbidden to keep a brothel or a gaming house'. That one I found in a book published in 1997 not, as that entry might suggest, 1897.

For Jethou I even resorted to the internet. To my surprise there were several pages of entries, a few referring to sailing in the Channel Islands, but nearly all on one subject; stamps.

In the 1950s and 60s, when Jethou was open to the public, stamps were issued to give publicity to the island. The lack of a good sandy beach, however (there is a stony one next to the slipway) meant that the island did not really catch on as a tourist attraction. When Guernsey and Jersey established their own postal systems in 1969, taking over responsibility from the British GPO, all such local stamps were banned.

On the internet, however, you can still buy them. How about the very first issue, a complete set of five from Jethou, Crevichon and Fauconnière, and featuring the druid stone, primroses, daffodils and bluebells? Mint (that's the condition not the herb) £48.99.

Strange that there should be no mention of the one plant peculiar to Jethou, a yellow forget-me-not. That fact was gleaned from *The Channel Islands* by Edith F Carey, first published in 1904 and possibly a little out of date by now.

THE BAILIWICK OF
JERSEY

JERSEY

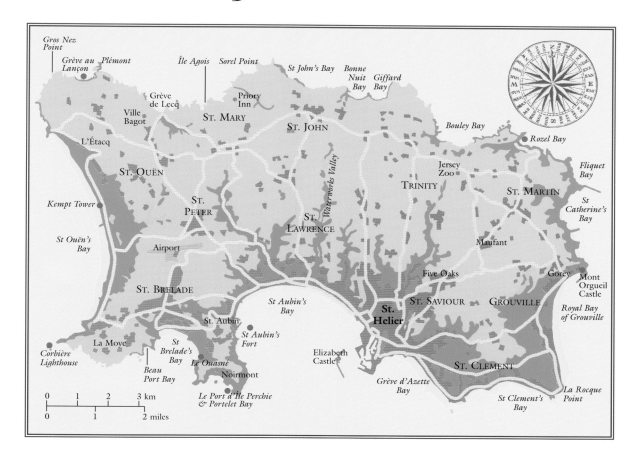

To refer to these islands collectively as the *Channel Islands* is to adopt a somewhat too British view of them. They are not even in the Channel, but the Gulf of St Malo. If we must perpetuate this attitude perhaps we should call them the *beyond-the-Channel Islands*. They are not so together as we mainlanders might think.

To an outsider, the way islanders regard the other islands can be both amusing and bemusing. "We don't mention that place" or "What do you want to go there for?" are often spoken with a smile or a chuckle that seem to be automatic responses born of a lifetime's practice, as if perpetuating a communal viewpoint which they know is really a myth. However, even when it is played down or denied altogether, you can still be left with a sense that there is a genuine streak of contempt running through some of these remarks.

Talking about Guernsey when on Jersey and vice versa can be particularly delicate. Sometimes I have referred to the "other island" as just that, and by doing so have been congratulated on my understanding of the situation.

There is a car sticker which reads *Guernsey – the thinking man's Jersey*.

While at sea Guernsey sailors consider it unlucky to mention Jersey, even if that is where they are bound.

On a good day you can just see Jersey from Guernsey, on a perfect one you can't see it at all.

People are all different of course and it is not difficult to find those with completely open minds on the subject, who see no reason for the islands to remain as independent from each other as they are at present and who find such attitudes puzzling.

While travelling around meeting local people, I have occasionally confessed a family connection, albeit distant, with Jersey. This usually engenders some sympathy or camaraderie depending on where the conversation takes place, but never indifference. I apologise to anyone from Guernsey who might be offended by that, but if you are I suppose that you would not be reading this chapter anyway.

My Jersey relations are by marriage and anglicised one generation. When I first knew them I knew nothing of the island, but slowly learnt many place names by overhearing reminiscences of childhood and holidays and looking through shoe boxes full of old photographs. The first place I heard about, and the location they all seemed to have a particular fondness for was Corbière. Naturally, when I visited for the first time it was top of my itinerary, if only to see what all the fuss was about.

The promontory of La Corbière is the southwestern corner of the island, exposed to the prevailing winds. It sits at the western end of the broad La Moye headland, which has at its eastern end the small but beautiful Beau Port Bay and between them two rather unglamorous neighbours, the prison and the desalination plant.

Corbière is exposed not only to the elements but to a great amount of publicity. It has become one of the symbols of Jersey, appearing on the island's 20p coin, seemingly every other postcard and the coach tour route. It is probably the most photographed location on the island and for that alone seemed to be the one place I should avoid painting.

The reasons for its popularity are twofold. It is

La Corbière Lighthouse

spectacular, but then so are many other places around this island. The difference is that it is accessible.

From the steep and twisting road that makes a circuit of La Moye, a concrete track leads down to the shore between two car parks and two German coastal defence bunkers, disappearing into the sea next to a Victorian villa which sits just above high water.

Beyond this point at high tide are innumerable pink/grey granite rocks which break up even a relatively calm sea into a foaming mass. On a windy day, when the sea churns, foams, sprays and thunders it is breathtaking.

At about half tide a causeway is exposed, along with much more of the granite, which has become rounded and sculpted by its constant battering from the sea. It is the perfect location for a low budget sci-fi film set on Saturn's moon Titan. At the end of this causeway – and here is the main attraction – on its natural rocky base about 500 metres offshore stands La Corbière lighthouse. Built by the States in only six months in 1873, it was the first lighthouse in the British Isles to be built of concrete, the materials being brought by ship as there was no road to the site at the time.

Do not venture out if you think a tour of the lighthouse is in the offing, conversion to automatic operation has left it unmanned.

The walk out to the lighthouse can usually be attempted below half tide. As with all water's edge activities, it is essential to check the tide times first. A bell sounds to warn of the rising tide, do not ignore it. The cross currents are very strong and people have died here, even a lighthouse keeper.

The rounded granite formations either side of the causeway are most inviting for those who enjoy a good clamber to get a different view, they are firm and have a fine texture which shoes grip well.

The name Corbière is derived from *corbeau*, the French for crow, traditionally a bird of ill omen and most appropriate here. The area has brought an early end to the working lives of many ships. Even as recently as 1995 the French ferry *St Malo* with more than 300 passengers on board made the news headlines all over Britain when it was holed attempting an inshore short-cut through the Jailers' Passage just beyond the lighthouse. On the headland a monument, a sculpture of two clasped hands, commemorates the rescue.

The Corbière headland is on the western edge of La Lande du Ouest, more commonly called Gorselands, a protected area of cliff top heathland rich in plant life especially, as is suggested by its name, gorse.

One plant however makes this area quite different from all similar heathland in the British Isles. Spreading carpets of an exotic looking plant flower in a variety of shades of pinks and yellows at the same time as the heath is covered in clumps of the more modest looking thrift, waves of quaking grass and with late flowering gorse. Its thick succulent leaves contrast with its more spiky neighbours.

Keen to know more I spoke to an Interpretation Officer for the States Environmental Services Unit at their Frances Le Sueur Centre in St Ouën. First of all

Hottentot figs at Corbière

I wanted to know what he interprets and for whom. He thought it was a rather grandiose title for someone who organises environmental education for primary schools – they have a classroom at the centre – and environmental awareness for islanders and visitors, including free guided walks Tuesdays and Thursdays from May to September. I think he is being modest.

The plant? It's the hottentot fig, introduced in about 1900 from South Africa and it's a pest. I told him that I thought it looked stunning. He agreed, but said that it's still a pest. It has become something of a problem as it takes over the habitat of native species and the nesting sites of birds, and can now be found on most of the south facing cliffs. The only natural halt to its advance is several nights of sharp frost, not much use as this has become something of a once-in-a-decade event. His Ranger colleagues occasionally organise work groups to pull the plant up. The working parties have been known to be attacked by handbag wielding old ladies objecting to this perceived floral vandalism. In my experience old ladies seem to think it's their right, as pensioners, surreptitiously to take cuttings of plants wherever they are, even National Trust properties and garden centres. Perhaps the hottentot's demise could be brought about by organising a gaggle of elderly ladies to roam the cliff tops taking cuttings.

I made detours to Corbière as often as I could, hoping to find an occasion when I felt moved to consider it paintable in order to pay tribute to the family that introduced me to the island. I finally succumbed to its charms early one autumn evening,

113

Beau Port - Bay

when a glorious golden dusk brought an unusually colourful end to an otherwise dull and breezy day.

East from Gorselands is the wonderful secluded bay of Beau Port. It is an unspoilt little bay with a small beach, sea-worn rocks and an offshore stack, all backed by red cliffs covered in what might be called a bit of wild Jersey: perfect for painting, bathing or just getting away from it all. I managed two out of three.

Beyond Beau Port is St Brelade's Bay. Broad, sandy and accessible, with hotels next to the beach and on the hillsides overlooking it. The bay is framed by two impressive headlands and the man-made contributions cannot distract from the glory of the natural setting. The bay is one of the most attractive parts of the island.

At the western end a slipway leads onto the beach which is overlooked by St Brelade's Church and its Fishermen's Chapel. Local boats tied to moorings shelter behind a small jetty. Close by at the foot of the sea wall many more are parked on trailers. If you want to know what happens to Jersey tractors when the come to the end of their farming lives, you will see that they are retired to St Brelade's beach to haul the boats out of the water.

At the eastern end of the bay more retired tractors are overshadowed by a cliff face that is an impressive 60 metres high wall of granite. Perched on the top a tiny white bungalow adds a dramatic sense of scale.

Round the corner from St Brelade's the fortified Noirmont headland overlooks another bay, Portelet, a mixture of its westerly neighbours, small but overlooked. The view is wonderful. In the bay sits a small islet, Île au Guerdian, on which stands a Martello tower. The island is the burial site of a ship's captain, Philippe Janvrin, who died of the plague and was not allowed to be buried ashore. At low tide Île au Guardian becomes part of the beach, so since 1721 the late Captain Janvrin has been coming ashore twice a day.

To the north of Corbière the landscape changes to the broad sweep of St Ouën's Bay. The cliff line appears to retreat a kilometre inland and a wide six kilometres long surf beach of hard sand links the framing granite headlands to the north and south enclosing a low lying coastal plain.

In theory this should be Sunset Strip. West coast California in miniature. Grand beach villas, drive-in ice cream parlours, sun-tanned surfers riding the waves by day, cruising a broad slab of tarmac in slinky dream cars after sundown. Thankfully it isn't, mainly due to the instability of the shifting sands. The surfers are here, at least at weekends. The ice cream parlours are of the soft-whip from a glazed Bedford van in the car park variety. As for showing off in chrome laden monsters from Detroit, the road is hardly wide enough to get two of them side by side and the 40 mph speed limit could seriously restrict the posing potential. The road, which runs the entire length of the bay just inland from the beach is known as Five Mile Road, but is in reality about three quarters of that in length.

There are apparently about 900 kilometres of road on Jersey. For an island only eight by fourteen and a half kilometres that seems an awful lot, but you

Le Port d'Île Perchie and Portelet Bay

do not get the impression that everywhere is covered in tarmac. There is one modest section of dual carriageway, from the centre of St Helier west round St Aubin's Bay. Most roads are rural country lanes, some are designated as Green Lanes, where priority is given to pedestrians, cyclists and horses, and where the speed limit is 15 mph. On these even 10 mph can feel a touch excessive. Five Mile Road is the longest, straightest road on the island, so visitors who feel the urge to slip into fifth gear while no-one is watching, this is your only chance.

On the whole St Ouën's Bay is natural and wild. It consists of flat marshy land, freshwater ponds, reed beds and sand dunes, all home to many rare and endangered species, some peculiar to Jersey. As well the great natural wealth, the historic remains of man's occupation of Jersey are also in abundance. Standing stones are many and Martello Towers and German defensive fortifications are prominent features along the beach head and offshore. The history of the island is here. If Jersey had a National Park this would be it.

Much of the area has been designated as a protected environ-ment and is carefully managed. In the south near Corbière are Les Blanches Banques, one of the largest dune systems in the British Isles, and to the north Les Mielles nature reserve.

Their natural appearance today is the result of restoration rather than preservation. The dunes were once considered perfect for car and motorcycle racing, Les Mielles a landscape once littered with derelict buildings and dumped rubbish. During the occupation many houses along the bay were demolished to make way for fortifications. If those that survived were the best, we had a lucky escape.

Now, nothing seems more natural than this restored landscape.

The conservation of the area is explained well at Kempt Tower, an interpretation centre built into one of the Napoleonic era defensive towers, where you can climb up to the roof for a panoramic view.

Joy with the Budget Car and some German concrete – St Ouën's

The fact that you are on a populous and industrious small island is only brought home when the quiet is broken by the aircraft passing overhead as they take off from the airport and the occasional vehicle passing along Five Mile Road.

It is easy to zip around the bay in a car and not take in its significance. The beauty is not in the grandeur of the scenery, but in the details, like the orchids and the skylarks. On a visit to Kempt Tower my eye was taken by its setting, which seemed to sum up well the nature of the bay. The grass and a solitary tree bending in the strong onshore wind, the geometry of the tower and a neighbouring German bunker, stout and solid.

At times like this I wish I could paint like Edward Hopper. The isolation of the location, the simple form of the buildings set in a natural landscape, even the blueness of the sky are so redolent of the images I have from him. Somehow he had the ability to simplify a scene, to remove all superfluous detail and yet produce a strong image which looked as if it really was like that, with nothing added, removed or even slightly altered. If I worked on his scale I know that I would end up painting every single blade of grass in sight and that is not really what I want. Working on a small scale has been my way of restraining that urge. My paintings are so small that it is simply impossible to put all the detail in, so over time I have developed a sort of shorthand for detail which gives the impression that it is all there.

St Ouën's Bay, particularly around L'Étacq at its northern end, is the most sparsely populated and 'old Jersey' area of the island, and one of the places you are most likely to come across that endangered species, an authentic Jersey accent. Although there are slight variations, on hearing one for the first time you would be forgiven for thinking it belonged to a native of South Africa, come to repatriate the hottentot fig. The beaming over from England of BBC and commercial television and radio stations is no doubt hastening its decline.

Also becoming rare, but because of its historical significance unlikely to become extinct, is Jerrais, the traditional spoken language of Jersey Norman-French, the Jersey patois. Writers have been stating since 1800 that the patois was falling daily into disuse, but it made something of a revival during the occupation because it was unintelligible to the Germans. It remained in common usage in the more rural areas until the 1960s but has declined since. Recently it has been introduced into schools as an optional subject for study while there are still people around to teach it.

The accent, I understand, sounds more natural in the context of the patois than in English.

As with the other islands, pronunciation of local place names can be a little unexpected.

Ouaisné (how many seven letter words contain all the vowels?) = way nay

Ouën = won (with o pron. as in *on*)

Catherine = Cath ryne

Voisins (a department store in St Helier) = Voy zins

Some odd pronunciation may originate with seasonal agricultural workers from Brittany who were once regular visitors to Jersey and had their own way of pronouncing place names.

Kempt Tower, St Ouën's Bay

The decline in the strength of the local language and the image the island has in some quarters of a flashy, go-getting playground for tax exiles from Britain, could give the impression that the traditional Jersey, as some would see it a rural land of potatoes and pretty cows, no longer exists. But it is still in abundance. If you fly here you only need to look out of the window as the runway is approached to see that the island is still mainly rural, a patchwork of small fields, hedgerows and attractive pink granite farmhouses.

Away from the south coast, this is the nature of much of the island. Small working farms, kilometres of dry stone walls, a liberal scattering of villages. It is an undulating landscape with plenty of trees, occasionally cut through by a series of densely wooded valleys that run southward from the higher ground in the north to St Aubin's Bay.

Herds of Jersey cattle will be found in the fields along with many examples of the Jersey vernacular, both linguistic and architectural, on the farms and in the villages. Occasionally the field pattern is interrupted by the often extensive grounds of a manor house. By contrast you also find the occasional lavoir, a communal trough where people once gathered to wash their clothes.

Some of the wooded valleys have been used over the last century for the creation of a number of reservoirs to provide drinking water for the island's expanding population. Some earlier examples of the exploitation of the water resources will also be found in the form of the surviving water mills. Two close together on the boundary of St Peter and St Lawrence parishes share the same water course and are particularly interesting. Le Moulin de Quétivel is leased from the Jersey New Waterworks by The Jersey National Trust which has restored it to full working order, producing stone-ground flour which can be bought at the mill. Down stream is the huge and impressive Tesson Mill, which has recently been bought by the Trust. They would like to restore that mill, too, if a sponsor and a sympathetic use for the building could be found.

A very fortunate and observant visitor may find that the valleys are also home to the red squirrel, sadly no longer a common sight on the mainland.

A local writer and journalist, and expert on all things Jersey gave me some good advice on finding the real island. Drive inland and every time you come to a junction, take the minor road. Eventually you will find yourself hopelessly lost, but you will have seen the genuine article. Try it in March and you will get the impression that this year's new crop is plastic sheeting. When I announced to a friend that I was about to start work on a book about the Channel Islands he sneered back, "The Channel Islands? Have you been? There's nothing to see, they're covered in polythene!"

Try it in April or May when the sheeting has been removed and you will see that virtually every field is crammed to the hedgerows with potatoes.

They must be the only potatoes to have their own website: www.jerseyroyals.co.uk.

Hitting the shops initially at four times the price of mere ordinary spuds, they may give the impression of being slightly over-priced. If that is your belief, the mistake you are making is thinking of them as just

potatoes. They are not called Royals for nothing, these are truly regal comestibles and should be treated with the dignity they deserve. Do not 'do things' with them, not even Duchesse potatoes is high enough up the culinary Civil List.

In our household they are received with the greatest reverence. For their initial banquet their royal highnesses will appear on a plate accompanied only by their ladies in waiting, Lady Seasoning and Lady Unsalted Butter. Hoi polloi, even the likes of the Duke of wild Skye salmon, are kept firmly in storage until another day.

Potato growing, as a commercial crop for human consumption, started in the early 1800s, about the same time as in Britain. The mild climate and the steep, south facing fields, côtils, enabled Jersey growers to produce a crop several weeks ahead of mainland farmers. Later in the century a number of factors combined to enable Jerseys to appear in the markets all over Britain much earlier. Competition

was the spur, also the need to beat the blight (which had spread through the USA and Europe mid century) along with swift, steam powered cargo ships and the spread of railways throughout Britain. The variety chosen then is still the one we buy today, a variant of the Jersey Kidney called the Fluke. However, the Jersey Royal Fluke, to give it its full name, is known everywhere else as the International Kidney.

The north of the island is where the potato is still king and the best place to soak up a bit of real Jersey countryside. It is a plateau of rural tranquillity, sitting between the wooded and urbanised valleys and the high, rugged northern cliffs.

My advice would be to sample it in May or October. The weather is usually mild and there are very few tourists about so the lanes are safer to use. They are not jammed with hire cars and the locals drive much more sensibly.

Buy a map. A local company called Perry's produce a good one, and the States reprint the

potato picking at St Ouen

1:25000 (4 cm = 1 km) Ordnance Survey Pathfinder, which is no longer available from the Ordnance Survey. It has every single field marked and is excellent. I find OS maps extremely useful. When working somewhere unfamiliar, time spent studying the map can save so much time otherwise wasted looking in the wrong places for an interesting subject. Even when not lost, I am lost without my OS maps.

Buy also a bus timetable, even if you are using a car to get around. Drive anywhere into the parishes of St John, St Mary or St Ouën, park the car somewhere sensible and get out and just walk. Once you get going you will not want to stop, certainly not turn round and retrace your steps, which is where the bus timetable comes in handy. Buses are also useful if you get lost or collapse from exhaustion or sensory overload. Walking is the most rewarding way of getting around, you notice the details that make the island different and it certainly makes it feel bigger.

It is surprising what you see sometimes. In one afternoon, only a short distance apart in St Ouën, I stumbled across two quite different pieces of Jersey's agricultural heritage, possibly unique in their field, no pun intended. I had been searching for a potato harvesting scene thinking that it might be a suitable subject for a painting. Next to the entrance to a field where I had been watching a potato harvester at work was a mediaeval stone-built sheep enclosure, a bergerie. Overgrown and barely visible, it needed a States information board, itself partially hidden by undergrowth, to point out that this was more than just a tumbled down section of granite field boundary. As in Britain, until the eighteenth century sheep were an essential part of the island's economy and bergeries were once a common sight. Sheep are something you do not see in Jersey any more and it needed sight of this bergerie to remind me of the fact.

Later, only a kilometre away and following a good lunch at Le Moulin de Lecq, which has no bearing on what follows, I noticed steam and smoke rising from behind a distant hedge. On investigation this was, as I suspected, a working traction engine, fired up and ready for action. On this occasion it was out having its photograph taken for the *Jersey Evening Post*.

It was strange coming across this at the ancestral home of my in-laws as this could have been a scene from my own family's history. Collyers once used equipment just like it to work the fields of rural Buckinghamshire, only a few kilometres to the north of Aylesbury where this particular engine had been built.

The north coast is the wildest part of Jersey's coastline and makes excellent walking country. I went in search of a view or two that said to me, Jersey – north coast. A well maintained footpath follows for the most part the cliff tops, with stunning views along the coast and, when visibility is good, out to sea. Access to the path is well signed and no doubt inexperienced ramblers are lured into trying it out. Fortunately the path is, on the whole, not too arduous and is liberally scattered with benches for the weary or overawed.

A hint for the authorities: for the benefit of non-residents, and those residents I have been amazed to

looking along north coast over the top of Île Agois

learn have never been here, the occasional discreet information panel, perhaps incorporated into the design of the benches – I know a very good designer/maker of 'public' furniture, I am sure it could be done – explaining the route and what may be encountered would be useful.

They do this well in Guernsey... that should spur them into action!

I recommend that you get hold of a copy of *Jersey Rambles* by John Le Dain (published by Seaflower Books). Walks are broken up into manageable chunks and the routes are well described: useful, as at times it is not always that clear which is the correct path to use even with a map.

Plémont, Grève de Lecq and Priory Inn make good starting points, comfort stops, or targets. Refreshments at the latter two are particularly good, there is plenty of parking and all three are bus route termini. Among the many splendid displays at the old Grève de Lecq Barracks Visitor Centre is information about the north coast footpath.

From Plémont there are good walks east and west. Here I was particularly taken with the steep descent to the beach. It looks innocent enough to begin with, then drops down to the sand or sea, depending on the tide, through a steep gorge. It was so dramatic I had to paint it. I chose a vertical composition to accentuate the drama of the gorge. The opportunity to paint a landscape that shape does not often arise.

It is important to be at a location at the right time. At midday in summer or on a damp, grey February morning it may not have looked impressive at all. I was lucky, arriving for the first time late one spring afternoon and finding the gorge in shadow, which added greatly to the drama of the descent. Although no artistic licence was used in portraying the scene, I managed to find a viewpoint which enabled me to avoid the steps and handrails which are a necessary safety feature of the path, but do nothing to enhance the view.

To the west from Plémont the footpath enters Les Landes, Jersey's largest area of maritime heathland and a Site of Special Interest. The marshland, gorse and heather are home to the rare Dartford Warbler and the Green Lizard, a Mediterranean native at the northern extent of its territory.

Les Landes covers the cliff tops around the Gros Nez headland, Jersey's north west corner, south to the inlet at Le Pulec which marks the northern end of St Ouën's Bay.

On the headland at Gros Nez are the remains of a fort about which little seems to be known. Historians say it is probably fourteenth century and is shown as a ruin on a sixteenth century map. I am sure they are right, but the setting is so perfect and the ruin so picturesque, mainly consisting of an archway forming part of a gatehouse, it looks suspiciously contrived to look good from someone's house. I suspect that really it is an eighteenth century gothic folly. Whatever it is, it's far too pretty to paint. Wouldn't I just be recycling someone else's handiwork?

To the south from here, the view takes in the huge slotted concrete drum of another German artillery lookout tower. Impressive as these buildings can often appear in their peculiarly sinister way, this

La Grève au Lanchon, Plémont

one is made to look insignificant by the splendour of the massive cliff face on which it stands.

On my north coast walkabouts I could not help noticing that although there were few tourists about a good number appeared to be from Germany. Curious, I mentioned this to my Jersey relatives who pointed out that there were quite a few here sixty years ago, too. Although only children at the time, they remember the occupation well and this prompted some reminiscences, particularly of the hardships it brought.

A curfew was introduced and people were shot for breaking it. All radios were confiscated so they were deprived of news, only being allowed information in German. Movement around the island was restricted. Diabetics died when the supply of insulin ran out as none could be obtained from Germany. All worthwhile items in the shops were bought up by the troops to send back to their families in Germany using Reichskredit, a worthless currency used only in occupied countries. This amounted to nothing more than looting by another name.

As some foods ran out they had to improvise, making coffee from parsnips, flour from potatoes and living almost entirely on swedes near the end when rations had been reduced to minimal levels: 25 grams of meat per person per week for instance. People, particularly the occupying soldiers, even resorted to eating pets. Garden gates disappeared overnight to be burned for fuel.

All births and deaths of farm animals had to be accounted for. To cheat the inspectors, when an animal died it would be passed round from farm to farm to be declared, thus creating 'spare' animals that could then be slaughtered to supplement the ration.

At the end, before Red Cross food parcels arrived, they were starving; the soldiers too.

On a lighter note, a doctor who brewed his own alcohol was caught in possession of some, but escaped punishment by convincing his inquisitor that it was a patient's urine sample.

An unfinished kilometre long network of tunnels, which were originally planned as an artillery barracks and stores and converted into a secure underground hospital when invasion from Europe looked likely, has been turned into a museum of the occupation.

A visit to this excellent museum is a very moving experience that I would recommend to anyone. Never before had I been to a museum so full of visitors where everyone moved around in silence and took so much care in studying the displays. The fact that this had occurred to a community that can so easily be identified with, and coming from a generation that has not endured anything like this at first hand, made for a profoundly chilling experience that will never be forgotten.

East from Plémont the cliff path to Grève de Lecq takes two short inland detours to negotiate the valleys of two streams and is here more undulating. In these valleys the flora and fauna change, the sounds of the wind and the sea are replaced by the babbling of the streams, the chattering of martins and the screech of the occasional swift.

On a clear day the other Channel Islands, particularly Sark, are best seen from along this stretch of coast. Offshore the Paternoster Rocks stand out dark and menacing. They were once considered such a hazard to shipping that sailors recited the Lord's Prayer to help their passage, hence the name *Pater Noster*; Our Father.

To some extent enjoyment of the various sections of the north coast path are dependent on whether you are looking for anything specific, or just out to blow the cobwebs away and clear your tubes. I was hoping to discover a striking piece of coastal scenery and arrived at Grève de Lecq without once being tempted to get out my sketch book.

While in Grève de Lecq time found to walk a short way up the hill towards St Ouën village will be well rewarded. Taking the first turning on the right, which has a no entry for vehicles sign, and following the narrow, damp and overhung lane to Ville Bagot, you will find a cluster of farmhouses, cottages and barns. Here is a piece of real Jersey hidden away so close to a popular holiday beach.

The westward walk to Grève de Lecq from Priory Inn might be found to be more rewarding than the eastward walk there from Plémont. The scenery is fabulous and in early summer the footpath is lined with a mass of wild flowers; foxgloves, ox-eye daisies, honeysuckle, cranesbill, vetch and many more competing with may blossom and the last of the gorse. It is a section of coast where the landscape is particularly good. The interaction of land and sea has resulted in some magnificent cliffs, rocky promontories occasionally pierced by caves and natural arches, and deep gullies where the cliff face is a 75 metres high, near vertical wall of granite. Most interesting of all is Île Agois, a small island separated from the adjoining cliff by such a narrow gorge that from many viewpoints it is impossible to tell that there is a gap at all. Archaeological evidence shows that there was once a religious settlement on the island.

Ville Bagot

In the vicinity of Île Agois or Devil's Hole near Priory Inn there are good views along the coast both east to Sorel Point and west to Plémont. On a bright hazy day, when the sky and sea appear to merge into each other and the distant headlands are just faint silhouettes devoid of detail, there is a marvellous sense of space for which the medium of watercolour is perfectly suited for capturing.

Further east along the north coast there is less of a sense of isolation. The cliff tops become more accessible by road, there are radio and television transmitter masts and a huge quarry, but there are also a number of pretty and popular bays.

My particular favourite is Rozel, a small cove surrounded by high wooded hills which come down to the sea on the south side of the cove. A harbour was constructed in the early part of the nineteenth century when the oyster trade was thriving. Rozel is a picturesque scene of working boats and pleasure craft nestling behind the harbour jetty, with attractive houses, restaurants, hotels and a gaggle of beach huts gathered behind a sea wall. Low tide exposes a rocky foreshore where ducks mingle with the usual gulls, but the roost is definitely ruled by a small number of vociferous geese.

If visibility is good the view from over the harbour wall is of the French coast in the vicinity of Carteret and, not so far off, the clutch of houses on Les Écréhous reef.

Just inland from Rozel is the place which many people around the world will only know Jersey for; the headquarters of the Durell Wildlife Conservation Trust, better known as Jersey Zoo. Set in the grounds of Les Augrès Manor, the zoological park was established in 1959 by the author and naturalist Gerald Durell. From the moment you enter it is quite clear that this is somewhat different, what zoo for instance would choose a dodo for its emblem? The answer is one that has set itself the task of saving animals from extinction by breeding endangered species in captivity with the aim of eventually reinstating them in the wild.

Rather than achieving this through captive breeding in the zoo itself, their aim is to establish recovery centres in the countries of origin with the zoo providing a genetic stock and undertaking programmes of education, training and research to help both the endangered animals and their habitats to survive and flourish.

Special emphasis is given to species that have been neglected by other conservation bodies, or those that might motivate the local people to help save them. Consequently the animal collection is very different from more conventional zoos and changes from time to time as conservation programmes begin or end.

Many of the animals I had not heard of; Giant Jumping Rats, Thick-billed Parrots, the Plumed Basilisk, for example. Some, I can safely say, I had not seen anything quite of their like before. For instance, imagine a cartoon ibis. A small black sphere with a burning fuse is thrown at its feet, it bends down to investigate and boom, there is an explosion and when the smoke clears the red faced bird looks up and blinks, its plumage fanned out and blackened; that is the Waldrapp Ibis, poor thing. Some are more attractive and that is sometimes an explanation for

Rozel Harbour

their plight, taken for the pet trade like the Bali Starling which, it would seem, is thriving if the zoo's own population is anything to go by, with many of the aviaries having examples flying about.

The grounds are over nine hectares of parkland and gardens with the animal enclosures placed apart from each other, giving an open and natural feel. Landscaping and planting has been designed to give the animals shelter and privacy and a sympathetic environment, using as much as possible plants native to their country of origin.

Cranes, flamingoes and waterfowl wander free in the shallow lakes and a natural stream bed and Andean Bears, Celebes Macaques, Lowland Gorillas and the highly entertaining Sumatran Orang-utans enjoy spacious paddocks with sheltered rest and play areas.

My particular favourites are the Livingstone's (of 'I presume' fame) Fruit Bats. One of the world's largest bats with a wing span of nearly two metres, they hang in their enclosure like fox-fur stoles tangled up in an umbrella stand.

If you become particularly attached to one species like I have, you can join their adoption scheme *SAFE* – Saving Animals From Extinction and help fund their recovery. A great day out that also contributes to saving wildlife, what more could you ask for?

The contrast between Jersey's north and south coasts could not be greater. It is difficult to believe that they are on the same small island only a few kilometres apart. To simplify geological matters greatly, imagine Jersey as a rectangular slab of granite tilted to the south to face the sun. In the north the land is lifted 100 metres above sea level creating the steep cliffs. From a northern cliff top plateau it then slopes southward, disappearing under the waves approximately eight kilometres away in St Aubin's Bay.

Between La Moye and Noirmont headlands in the south west and Gorey on the east coast, the southern coastline of Jersey is, with the exception of the rock strewn south east corner, wide sandy bays backed, it seems, by most of the hotels on the island. This is not only holiday Jersey. I would think that a majority of the island's residents live within sight of, or at most a modest walk from this coast.

From the buildings overlooking the causeway leading to St Aubin's Fort, to those nestling beneath the ramparts of Mont Orgueil Castle, a distance of about 19 kilometres, the coastal strip is more or less one continuous built-up area, varying greatly in its nature and appearance.

To the east of St Helier along the coast road to La Rocque at the south east corner of the island and round into Grouville on the east coast, a visitor from England would feel very much at home. There is a definite air of a traditional, well-kept English seaside town in both the architecture and colour of the buildings.

It is beyond the sea wall, off Grève D'Azette and St Clement's Bay – and where the architect is mother nature – that this corner of the island remains characteristically Jersey. There is an other-worldliness about the large area of rock ledges that extend three kilometres offshore. This is one of the locations along the island's south coast where the huge tidal range has its most dramatic effect. Without doubt, the fundamental changes brought about all along these southern shores by the ebb and flow of the sea is the most striking feature this side of Jersey.

The tidal range is one of the greatest in the world, up to 10 metres, and the appearance of some locations changes dramatically. When the tide is out places like Seymour Tower, Elizabeth Castle and St Aubin's Fort, surrounded by sea for half the day, suddenly become somewhere you can walk to. There is a strange thrill to walking along the causeway to Elizabeth Castle knowing that soon this will once again become the sea bed.

So extensive is the area of firm sand exposed at low tide in St Aubin's Bay, that in the days before the airport was built it served as the runway for Jersey Airways, tides permitting.

Whether the tide is rising or falling is an important factor to consider when making a journey. If you stroll out from La Rocque a warning bell will not sound at Seymour Tower to let you know that you are about to be cut off for six hours by the tide.

Time can slip by quickly when you are concentrating on finishing a painting. To ensure that I am always aware of how much time I have to work at a particular spot I acquired a Tidemaster watch, an ingenious device designed initially for sailors and divers, but very useful in the Channel Islands if you are in the habit of visiting the offshore sites.

Basically it is a good quality watch, with the addition of a rotating outer bezel. This is marked to indicate the state of the tide; high, low etc and all you do is rotate the bezel to the time of the next high or low tide so that at a glance it shows you how much time there is to go; wonderful. It has proved to be most useful when I have been working at one location and need to be at another at a certain state of the tide later in the day. It has been so helpful in organising my working days I could not manage without it.

La Rocque was the site of a French invasion in 1781 resulting in the Battle of Jersey. A plaque commemorating the event is sited on the sea wall below a grand turreted and dormered Edwardian house. Next to this is one of the many Jersey Round Towers that were built along this low lying and vulnerable stretch of coast following the battle. You can spot them along the coast road to Grouville, but

Jersey Round Tower — Grouville Bay

Mont Orgueil Castle, Gorey

a safer and more enjoyable way to view them is from the sea wall or the beach. Some are free standing while others have been incorporated into houses, looking like elaborate extensions built by someone with an interest in military history and a sense of humour.

North from La Rocque is the rather grandly named Royal Bay of Grouville. Grouville village is for the most part set back from the sea. At the northern end of the bay is Gorey, a village almost falling off the hillside into the sea. The bay and Gorey village are dominated by the fabulous Mont Orgueil Castle, built after 1204 when the Duchy of Normandy was lost to France. Set upon a granite mound from which it appears to have grown naturally, the castle towers over the village and its harbour and is a great tourist attraction . . . and no wonder.

My friendly authority on all local matters, lucky man, has a house close by the castle and persuaded me that something about Jersey would be incomplete without it. After explaining that one of the rules I try to follow when choosing a location at which to work is 'avoid the obvious', he told me about the small bay immediately to the north of the castle, Le Petit Portelet. It is seldom visited and the view of the castle is quite different from the one most people will be familiar with. For this I was thankful.

Unlike castles of this age and size on the mainland, which are mostly ruins, this is as complete as if it had only just been finished. So apparently useful it still appeared to be, it was modified during the German occupation. Had I not had this pointed out to me I may not have noticed. Three round

observation towers were added, faced with local granite so they blend in with the rest of the building. You cannot see the join. Having seen many of their other structures, and heard about life during the occupation, this shows a surprising degree of sensitivity.

Driving along the coast road west from St Helier round St Aubin's Bay, it is impossible to tell whether you have left the town or not; Millbrook, Beaumont, you cannot see the join here either. As St Aubin is approached there is one small break in the buildings. The village appears to be separated from the spread of the exotic suburbia from St Helier by a field of fancy lettuces.

St Aubin is a good place to be. There's a little harbour, an offshore Tudor fort, Fort George, that can be reached on foot at low tide, the old cobbled high street, La Rue du Crocquet that looks more French than anywhere else on the island.

I enjoy staying in St Aubin, especially at the Mont de la Rocque Hotel, perched high up overlooking the whole sweep of St Aubin's Bay. It is always so welcoming and comfortable and, a good sign, has the same staff every visit. Finding it was one of those good pieces of fortune that come about quite by chance.

Do we want to stay in St Helier? Not really. It would be nice to get away from the bustle of the town. And if I wanted to go somewhere, to do a little work before breakfast maybe, I wouldn't want to fight my way through early morning traffic or have to walk too far. It would have to be somewhere much smaller and more Jersey-like. To be able to tell if the

The view was wonderful. The view was painted. The changing view is fascinating.

Breakfast and dinner take so long to finish because so much time is spent just staring out of the window at *that* view. The coming and going of the tide, people riding horseback on the sand, *Condor* arriving from Poole, oystercatchers noisily being oystercatchers. The food is always excellent, imaginative and well presented. The goat cheese hors d'oeuvre is worth the trip alone. Recommended for fishyphiles is the menu entirely made up of lobster dishes. The tables are always busy, even out of season, which suggests that it is a popular place with the locals. I love it.

Eating out in Jersey is always a joy, it is where the essential

La Rue du Crocquet St. Aubin

light and tide are right for working I would need somewhere with a good sea view of course. How about somewhere overlooking St Aubin? It's a nice village with a harbour. The Mont de la Rocque is high up and has rooms with sea views and balconies. Alan Wicker says it's one of the finest views he's ever seen. That's a pretty good endorsement, he must have seen some good views in all his travels. We'll give them a try shall we? You never know, the view might make a good painting...

Englishness of the island really takes on a French flavour, literally. In terms of art this would be akin to the blend of influences and ideas that became L'Art Nouveau. The British gave it a French name and visit Guernsey or Jersey for a hint of France. Paradoxically the French sometimes refer to it as Le Style Anglaise and visit the Islands for a taste of Britain.

In Don Street, St Helier there is an exquisite Art Nouveau door handle. The deceptively simple sinuous curve is perfection in brass. If it had been designed by Louis Sullivan it would resemble a small sculpture of a briar rose, twisting round a ruined archway of a long neglected abbey. And you would probably not recognise it for the door handle it was meant to be. If it had been designed by Antoni Gaudí it would shout (in Catalan of course) 'don't touch me, I'm a precious work of art' as you approached. Thankfully it is neither of these. It is a supreme piece of design, elegant and attractive yet honest with it, performing its task brilliantly. Happy to be a great door handle, it does not slap you round the face with a copy of *Pioneers of Modern Design* as you grip it and push the door open.

I would recommend you seek out this door handle and

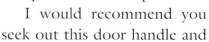
Art Nouveau door handle – Bistro Central

do just that, grip it gently, give it a push and step through. Inside you will find yourself in the culinary equivalent of that door handle, this too has a French name, Bistro Central. The flavour is as Parisian as Hector Guimard's Métro station entrances, with the emphasis on local seafood. Even the most ardent fishyphobes would find their appetites ever so slightly whetted. The menu offers:

SUPREME de FLETAN 'BASQUAISE'
grilled supreme of halibut, black olive and garlic crust
stew of tomatoes and peppers

BROCHETTE FRUITS de la MERE à la CHINOISE
grilled seafood kebab, including scallops and king prawns
vegetable stir-fry, hoi sin and ginger jus, timbale of rice

PAUPIETTES de LIMANDE FARCIE 'ST. GERMAINE'
steamed fillets of lemon sole, pea puree, crisp bacon lardons
red wine and thyme sauce

FILET de LOUP de MER à l'ORIENTALE
baked fillet of sea bass, szechuan pepper, oriental vegetable broth
crispy noodles

FILET de SAUMON 'BELLE PRINCESSE'
crisped salmon fillet, asparagus garnish; chive hollandaise

MEDAILLONS de LOTTE et COQUILLES 'CENTRAL'
saute of monkfish and scallops, black pudding and apple garnish, herb butter

SUPREME de CABILLAUD à l' ITALIENNE
roasted pancetta-wrapped cod fillet
chunky provençal compote, parsley mash

As and when available
FRESH DOVER SOLE, TURBOT and BRILL

Divine!

I ate there one busy Saturday night with friends old and new, from England and from Jersey. The next evening presented something of a problem as it was a Sunday out of season. Sadly, Le Mirage Bistro at Mont de la Rocque Hotel was closed, the only place we knew that could be relied upon to produce an equally good evening without seeming second best to the delights of the previous night. We chose instead a noted restaurant overlooking the harbour in St Aubin. It featured in the long running television detective drama series *Bergerac*, which broadcast pictures of the beautiful Jersey landscape into millions of British homes every Sunday night during the '70s. It came with many recommendations from friends and family, so was thought to be a safe bet.

Unfortunately our experience was the complete opposite of the previous night. Service was poor, some of the food was not as described on the menu, one course was almost inedible and the order for another forgotten altogether. Our complaints went largely unanswered. Strangely it was quite clear that other diners at a nearby table had eaten there the night before; obviously gluttons for punishment rather than good food.

It was pointed out by a member of our party that I was to be interviewed live on BBC Radio Jersey the next morning and might be tempted to relate these experiences to the populace. The beauty of a live broadcast is that there is no opportunity for editing. From mouth to radio audience in milliseconds. Even this threat went unheeded.

For the next few days I had very little appetite, probably a touch of food poisoning.

I chose not to mention our experience on the fleeting medium of the airwaves. Print is so much more permanent I feel.

The saga continues.

Before breakfast two days later we witnessed, from the comfort of our hotel room, a dramatic incident in St Aubin's Bay. The tide was high and a strong southwesterly wind was creating a choppy surface, it was grey, wet and stormy.

A small launch from St Aubin's harbour had put two men aboard cruisers moored in the bay, presumably in preparation for moving them to their winter moorings inside the harbour. As it started to make for the quay at St Aubin's Fort we saw a bright orange distress flare fired from across the other side of the bay in the direction of Elizabeth Castle.

Through binoculars I could see a yacht struggling against the elements, pitching and rolling and occasionally disappearing in the troughs between waves. The launch, which I would have thought was not the most suitable vessel itself for such conditions, changed direction and headed out across the bay to the rescue, along with another boat from St Helier. Eventually the yacht was brought under tow into St Aubin's harbour.

That evening the rescue was one of the main stories on Channel Television's evening news programme. Apparently the three young crew members, who were all inexperienced sailors, had recently purchased the vessel and were moving it from St Helier to St Aubin in the less than ideal conditions. After leaving St Helier their engine had

St Aubin's Fort, low tide

Mont de la Rocque with St Aubin's Bay

failed and they were becoming swamped. None of them knew how to put up the sails. Fortunately one of them at least knew how to fire a distress flare. They looked dishevelled but relieved to be ashore.

Watching the television news report of an event that I had witnessed at first hand felt a little odd, it was something I had not experienced before. For the moment our curiosity had been satisfied.

The following day, still feeling a little queasy, I paid a visit to the Harbour Office in St Helier to say hello to friends who are responsible for managing the marina there. Eventually the conversation came

140

round to the fact that I had witnessed the early morning drama of the previous day. This was greeted with raising of eyebrows and rolling of eyes. Among the tuts and groans a sentence was uttered that brought a smile to our faces,

"They were three young chefs from that restaurant in St Aubin."

They got their just desserts.

Traditional Jersey fare is unlikely to appear on a restaurant menu, although items such as lobster and spider crab will always be a favourite. Naturally many specialities from the surrounding waters, or from the sand at low tide were once a major part of the diet; conger eel made into soup, ormers, sand eels, razor fish and oysters. Bean crock, a casserole made from mixed beans, pork and beef is similar to the French dish cassoulet. Before the potato came to take over the fields the main crop was apples and cider was a major export. Black butter, a preserve made with cider, apples, sugar, lemons and liquorice is still found on sale in small local shops and the Victorian Central Market in St Helier.

This is also one of the very few places where my particular favourite is still available, the donut-like Jersey Wonders. I have a distant cousin who is one of the top pastry chefs on the island, this is her recipe which was given to her by an elderly Jersey lady whose family kept an inn at Le Carrefour Selous:

400g self-raising flour
100g caster sugar
100g butter
3 eggs

Cream the butter with the sugar. Add the eggs. Kneed in the flour. Roll out to about 2 cm thick – no more – and then cut into rectangles about 5 x 7 cm, about 20. In each piece cut a diagonal slit about half of the way across from top left to bottom right corners. Take the other two corners and pass them through the slit. Leave them to rest on a tray for half an hour while you put your feet up and have a nice cup of tea. Deep fry them until they are a deeper than golden brown, then flip them over and to cook on the other side. Drain on kitchen paper. Best eaten warm before anyone else discovers you have made them. They are good just as they are or coated in icing sugar, cinnamon, or nutmeg, or with jam, or to be really decadent, dipped in Jersey cream.

Tourism and agriculture are no longer the mainstays of the Jersey economy. Like Guernsey it is now dependent on financial services, but somehow that does not come as a surprise. The quality of the houses and cars, the boats in the marina, the goods in the shops, the way people dress, all let you know that there's plenty of money sloshing around. Most of the income that supports these things is generated from the offices concentrated in downtown St Helier. As money talks, I will let it fill you in itself on the details in the way it does best; with lots of numbers.

Jersey's gross domestic product is £1.35 billion. Agriculture accounts for a modest 5% of that, tourism 24% and financial services 55%. The finance industry employs approximately 10,000 people, that is one in eight of the population. There are 79 banks, with deposits of about £100 billion (I would put that as a one followed by 11 zeros). There are 33,000

Elizabeth Castle, low tide

companies registered in Jersey, that is two companies for every five residents.

Despite its wealth-generating offices and smart looking banks – the new Royal Bank of Scotland building is particularly fine – St Helier, it has to be said, is not quite as attractive as the rest of the island. There is a modern working port and sea-borne visitors are welcomed by the paraphernalia that goes with it, warehouses, oil storage tanks and the like, and a power station with a huge chimney. And why not? There is nothing wrong in that. Jersey is not a playground, work has to be done, power generated and it has to happen somewhere, so why not concentrate it in St Helier on land largely reclaimed from the sea? It's just that when you have taken in the rest of the island, it all brings you back down to earth with a bit of a bump.

The problem is, I suppose, that the rest of the island is so marvellous. Almost anywhere would look a trifle ordinary and workaday by comparison. It looks, dare I say it, like somewhere in England. Blocks of flats, a road tunnel, multi-storey car parks, a one way system that stumped even my usually good sense of direction. And forget trying to park!

The town centre is a shopaholic's dream. Take away all the jewellers and perfumeries taking advantage of the VAT-free status and you are still left with a shopping centre most county towns would be happy with, including two splendid department stores and, architecturally, a Boots to knock the others flat. Most wonderful of all though is the Victorian Central Market building, a grand affair of glass and painted iron; the Crystal Palace meets

Bristol Temple Meads to sell fruit and vegetables and much more besides.

I have been to many maritime museums around Britain, varying greatly in their size, scope and ambitions. Some carry it off better than others. The most impressive was Aberdeen's, a modern structure reflecting the industry it concentrates on most, North Sea oil. The new one on the quayside in St Helier is even better; wide ranging, enjoyable and a feast for the eyes. Everyone involved in putting it all together should be very proud of themselves. It is very hands-on and interactive, but not gimmicky, bringing out the child-like sense of wonder that lurks within us all.

Constructed within a group of Edwardian quayside warehouses, the exhibition spaces are on a number of levels providing variety and the joy of discovery. The emphasis is not on a dry collection of objects needing extensive textual explanation, but a visual cornucopia portraying journeys, events, people, trades and sea life in general, brought together with stories and shanties. Old salts will still find lots of sepia photographs and bits of old boats to look at and another old salt or two to reminisce with.

St Helier is a fairly concentrated collection of buildings. Open spaces like parks and squares do not abound, though they do exist, somewhere. On the other hand, only a short walk from the commercial centre of town is the sea wall with a pretty good view of the Atlantic Ocean. If that is not a big enough open space for you I would suggest you get that claustrophobia looked at. After a stressful day at the office what more could you ask for to relieve the

Le Ouasné beach

tension than a stroll out along the causeway to Elizabeth Castle? The tide to be out, maybe?

From all angles Elizabeth Castle makes a picturesque sight. With its towers and corner turrets, a unifying outer wall and sitting astride two small rocky islands, at low tide it looks like a giant sandcastle.

The fortification of the site began in the mid sixteenth century when it became clear that the development of cannons and gunpowder made the mediaeval Mont Orgueil Castle less formidable and there was a need to have a site out of range of these new weapons. The castle is a complex of buildings developed over a period of 250 years and added to during the German occupation.

The main gate is approached up a slipway used by the amphibious vehicles which carry visitors when the sea covers the causeway. To the right of the slipway is the seventeenth century former outpost Fort Charles, incorporated into the main castle wall at a later date.

Once inside it becomes clear that the castle is divided into three distinct areas or wards.

The Outer Ward is a mainly open grassed area built on the smaller of the two islands, with a hospital and workshops dating from 1800 and all enclosed by seventeenth century walls containing a number of defensive positions. From here a bridge spans the ditch which is the remains of the storm beach that separated the two islands, and leads into the Lower Ward on the larger island.

This large space was the parade ground and is surrounded by a number of barrack blocks which now house museum displays and a cafe. A cross in the parade ground marks the site of a church destroyed by an explosion during bombardment of the castle in the English Civil War when gunpowder was stored in the crypt.

The Upper Ward is the original castle, named Fort Isabella Bellissima – after his Queen, the most beautiful Elizabeth – by Jersey's Governor Sir Walter Raleigh. On this site is The Mount, the highest part of the island and the first defensive work, which became a German fire control tower during the occupation. Next to the mount is the Governor's House, built in 1590.

Beyond the Upper Ward a nineteenth century breakwater leads out to the rock where in the sixth century a hermit Helier or Helerius lived in a cave. The son of a Belgian nobleman, he went to Jersey for solitude and became famous for his powers of healing and was eventually canonised. To commemorate him an oratory was built in the twelfth century on the site which is now called the Hermitage.

I could get to like it here. I think I could just about cope with St Ouën's Bay, the north coast cliff top footpath, or strolling out to Seymour Tower to walk off a particularly good Dover Sole.

Getting to live here presents something of a problem, however. If my work was considered to be an essential job, I may be let in for a temporary stay, a few years, possibly renewable. Only a handful of wealthy people are allowed in each year for a permanent residency. They have to convince the States chief executive of their good character along with the small matter of their ability to pay a minimum of one hundred thousand pounds in tax each year.

Farms at L'Ètacq

I could avoid all that and stay indefinitely if I became someone's lodger and did not have my own front door key (allowing free access by my landlord) and was not the sole user of my kitchen. It does happen and I have heard that visits from landlords and other kitchen users are a little thin on the ground, if you get my meaning. The rent is a bit steep, though.

If I was single I could find a Jersey bean (as the locals are known) to marry. We would have to stay together for ten years and then I would become a resident. It's as easy as that.

I think I will have to wait for a total collapse of the world's banking system or, perhaps, just visit more often. The problem is with each visit it becomes harder to face going home.

On my working visits, with one exception, I have flown, and always with KLM (UK). In the interests of equality it has enabled me to remain neutral as they are a Dutch company. It seems to me to make good business sense for the Islands to have them as there is, through Schiphol (Amsterdam) airport, a link into the international network; putting the Channel Islands on the world flight map. By KLM it was possible to fly from Jersey to New Jersey, New Jersey being named after Jersey when it was given by Charles ll and James, Duke of York to their Jersey supporters after the Civil War.

I am indebted to KLM for the inspiration for my book title *South by Southwest*. This is the direction one needs to travel from my home to reach these Islands. Checking in at Southampton for the first time I noticed that next to the KLM logo there was also that of their American partner airline Northwest. Being an admirer of the work of both Alfred Hitchcock and Cary Grant it brought to mind that

great film of theirs *North by Northwest*. To re-work such a well known title seemed to make good sense and had a hint of my previous book about it.

Using both KLM and Northwest it was possible to fly from Jersey to Rapid City South Dakota, where Cary Grant was taken (by Northwest) in the build-up to the film's climax.

Soon after deciding on the title I made another trip to Jersey. Returning to my hotel one morning after a pre-breakfast sketching trip to Ouaisné Bay, I turned on the car radio and out came Bernard Hermann's title music for *North by Northwest*. At the time I was driving into St Aubin down a steep wooded valley with hairpin bends, reminiscent of the Riviera in another Hitchcock/Grant film *To Catch a Thief*. The music fitted the drive perfectly. On returning to my hotel I related this to Joy who by coincidence had at the same time reached the making of *North by Northwest* in Graham McCann's biography of Cary Grant, *A Class Apart*. This was confirmation if I needed it that the correct title had been chosen.

If Jersey could be personified I think it would have to be Cary Grant; English, but only just. Debonair, polished, professional, with a touch of romance, but somewhere deep down, still Archie Leach.

PLATEAU DES MINQUIERS

Les Minquiers is a 65 kilometres reef lying 17 kilometres south of Jersey. In clear weather it is visible from there, sitting just on the horizon. At high water it is a collection of isolated rocks. At low water it is an archipelago larger than Jersey. The name apparently comes from the French word for a fish wholesaler *minque*.

Originally our plan was to visit the Minkies – as they are known locally – for the day while on a working visit to Jersey; the Minkies on Friday, the Écréhous on Sunday. It all seemed so straight forward. The offer to organise the visits came from friends in the Jersey Harbour Office.

I was to be taken there in an Aqua Star *Barbarella B* by its owner, a retired ships' captain, former Jersey harbour pilot and lifeboat coxswain. His knowledge of the waters around the islands in all their various states is encyclopaedic. With his more than 50 years sailing experience and still teaching navigation, I would be in the safest hands possible.

No problem.

Cometh the day, cometh the wind. It was far too risky.

He must have sensed my disappointment over the phone when he informed me that the trip was off and suggested a meeting at the Yacht Club for a chat over coffee instead. Within a few minutes of meeting I was offered the chance of staying on the Minkies. I was in the presence of someone who actually owned a property there.

looking up from the shore

149

Momentarily I was stunned. Stay on the Minkies? Overnight? Me? On my own?

For once my imagination failed to produce a picture of what that might entail. It did not equate with anything stored in my memory bank.

"I assume Joy will be going as well, you'll be wanting your home comforts!"

With pride he flourished an album of photographs documenting the four year rebuilding of his property from a gable end or two poking out from a pile of rubble into a single storey cottage.

"How long would you want to stay?"

"A couple of nights?"

"You'll need at least three to get a feel for the place."

"Three it is then."

"It's a difficult place to get into. There are lots of submerged rocks and the level drops about eleven metres on a spring tide, so the water runs fast through the channels. It's a dangerous place if you're not familiar with it. To see the full effect of the changes in levels for your work we would need to get you there on a spring tide, arriving at about half tide down. It takes two hours to get there so we must leave St Helier at about an hour after high tide."

This is when it began to dawn on me that visiting the Minkies might be a bit of an adventure even in favourable weather.

After consulting diaries and tide tables we opted to set off from St Helier at 8 am on Monday 12th July.

Two hours in a comfortable force 3 brought us to our destination, tying up at the States of Jersey mooring buoy.

Immediately to our west was the appropriately named main 'island', Maîtresse Île, a granite protrusion of probably no more than 100 metres in length and 15 to 20 metres in width, supporting a slipway, a flag pole, a helicopter pad, seven small habitable buildings and four ruined ones and, doubling as a sea mark (you line it up with the chimney pot on the building behind it to bring yourself safely to the buoy), the most southerly building in the British Isles; the communal lavatory.

At the top of the slipway visitors are greeted by the States of Jersey Customs House. Naturally this, too, is the most southerly of its kind in the British Isles. It is kept unlocked as a haven for shipwrecked sailors – with a fair chance of being used I would think. Inside there are five beds, but only one pillow, a table and stool, a bright blue tarpaulin, a candle in a bottle and a substantial fireplace fitted with a very nice Victorian cast iron range which would finish off my dining room back home perfectly. Visitors are expected to leave some provisions for the poor shipwrecked sailors. On the table was a tin of baked beans, but no can opener, and a packet of Safeway Slim Choice Asparagus Soup with Croutons. Slim choice indeed.

The collection of buildings are former fishermen's huts, probably from the nineteenth century although building work has revealed several different floor surfaces below the most recent, suggesting renewal over a long period of time. Dwellings of some sort must have been here in about 1800 as there are stories of the dispute between the semi-resident fishermen and the quarrymen who came here for

150

View across Les Minquiers

granite for Fort Regent in St Helier. The fishermen were angry that too much granite was being removed and threw the quarrymen's tools into the sea.

There is something unnatural about being on the Minkies. The wildlife seems very at home, but somehow I get the impression that man was not designed for this.

Soil is almost non-existent so very little grows, certainly nothing you would consider eating except in the most desperate circumstances. Mallow grows well and, I understand, makes a good substitute for toilet paper, being as soft as a baby's bottom and it adds a splash of colour when in flower.

We brought food for four, gastronomically speaking, carefully planned days. If the weather turned foul and we could not be taken off for some time we may have been in trouble, but we did at least have a can opener. Sea birds are plentiful, so I guess that we could have turned fowl, too. I have eaten braised puffin and very nice it was, but our first mate, appropriately dressed in a Jane Fonda as Barbarella tee-shirt, informed us that "the birds round here don't have much meat on them," which I took to be a reference to the gulls and cormorants.

Water for most purposes must be brought over in barrels or bottles, although in some instances wine and beer can be used as an alternative. The communal toilet is flushed with sea water from a bucket. This is easy to fill from a rock pool at low tide, but at high tide involves a dash down the slipway to catch a wave. It certainly makes you appreciate the convenience of running water and drains. I see now why the Victorians celebrated the arrival of clean and healthy water systems by building their waterworks to look like grand Italianate palaces.

Our home for four days was to be a little more modest. Boarded for protection against the weather and light fingered visitors, our four granite walls housed kitchen, dining room, lounge and bedroom in open-plan style. Reconstruction was based on the foundations of two separate dwellings and still had to conform to the planning requirements of the Jersey parish of Grouville; of which the Minkies form an outpost and to which the owners of the various properties pay rates. These understandably are at a reduced level as they do not receive all the regular services of the parish, street lighting and refuse collection for instance.

The buildings are surrounded by a low wall of granite blocks, which is interrupted only where nature has provided her own sea defence. At the highest tides all but the top of the slipway is covered and the sea almost reaches the wall, showering the huts with spray when the wind blows strong. A walk round the block, excluding the helicopter pad, takes little more than a minute. If you move fast enough it is possible to get all of the landed sea birds in the air at the same time; quite a sight and a sound.

Looking out to sea, the northern horizon is dominated by Jersey. To the east, if visibility is particularly good, is the pale silhouette of the Normandy coast in the vicinity of Coutainville and to the south east France's equivalent of the Isles of Scilly, Îles Chausey. Close by the sea is broken only by the occasional rock, with four small outcrops about 200 metres to the east, each supporting a pilotage beacon.

Low tide brings a dramatic change of scenery.

The retreating sea reveals massive granite boulders, smooth and rounded by the action of the sea, which help to protect the island by dissipating some of the energy of the waves. The four offshore outcrops of rock are transformed into the peaks on a mountain range maquette. All around the sea is filled with a maze of pink/beige granite outcrops, which to the west stretch to the horizon, appearing to be more rock than sea. Most spectacular of all, a huge curving golden beach of shell fragments is revealed. The scale is difficult to comprehend until the tiny specks that appear on it are revealed through binoculars to be gulls.

Particularly low tides are known locally as ormering tides. A great delicacy, the ormer is a large Mediterranean cousin of the limpet, found here at the northern extreme of its habitat and under rocks

the most southerly building
in the British Isles

exposed at low water. The Minkies is a good place to fish for them as their relative inaccessibility has prevented the over fishing that has occurred round the populous islands. The gathering of them is strictly controlled. It may only take place between September 1st and April 30th, and then only on the first day of each new moon or full moon and the three following days, and only if the shell is a minimum of eight centimetres long. Possession of them is allowed for a further two days beyond the four fishing days. After that you are in deep water, so to speak.

On the rock there isn't total silence, but it's close to it. The gentle crash of waves on rocks and the raucous laughter of hundreds of gulls soon fade into the background. The distant drone of a boat's engine is instantly picked out as something unnatural.

While one of the senses enjoys something of a holiday, another goes into overdrive. At times the smell of what is politely known as guano can be overpowering, but you soon learn to stand or sit somewhere else.

We lounge in soporific splendour. The sea rises, the sea falls. From their roof-top perches the great black backed gulls taunt the herring gulls on the rocks below who squawk back, they know their place and don't like it. Cormorants and shags stand around in small groups as if waiting for a bus to come along. Common terns squabble over sand eels as a group of oystercatchers circle as if preparing to perform a Red Arrows display. A mating pair of clown face beetles shunt back and forth across a rock.

It's another hectic day at the Minkies.

If your appetite has been whetted, I understand that one property is on the market for a modest £15,000. There are two drawbacks, however. Firstly you must be a Jersey resident and meet their house purchasing regulations. Secondly, the property is a gable end and a pile of rubble, but it's a start, and you won't have many interruptions while you work.

LES ÉCRÉHOUS

As we gathered on the quayside at Gorey Harbour on a cool Sunday morning in mid May, a light drizzle fell. To the south, the broad sweep of the Royal Bay of Grouville faded away into the greyness. This was more hot bacon rolls than ice cream weather.

"They say it's going to brighten up later."

How many times was I to hear that? We were reassured however by the amount of activity in the harbour. Hardly the bustling masses, but even if these few people believed that it really was going to . . . then it must be true.

One theory I have heard propounded in the Harbour Office is that, in general, the weather is fair with a spring tide and not with a neap. In this instant it was true, we were on a neap and it's just not fair.

It was touch and go whether we made the trip at all. If there was not the need to get me there it would probably not have been considered as a possibility. A force 4 was blowing from the south west, so at least we would be in the lee of Jersey and after all, it was going to . . .

We set off more in hope than expectation in our Mitchell Sea Angler *Tamalou*. My chaperons for the trip were *Tamalou*'s owner, a retired pilot for the Gorey ferries who now keeps himself busy with spider crab and prawn pots, a bit of diving and generally being very useful around the harbour, my Miss Fix-it who is also the manager of Marine Registrations at the Harbour Office in St Helier and her father, at various times Commodore of St Catherine's Sailing Club, Captain of Gorey Regatta Association and, most impressive of all, builder of two Mirror dinghies in his dining room next to the grand piano. I felt seriously under qualified to hold conversation with such knowledge-able companions.

Jersey's grey outline soon began to disappear into the drizzle and for a while we were out of sight of both our departure point and destination as we headed north east on our nine kilometre journey.

first view from the boat

With nothing much to see beyond the boat my attention turned to the cabin where I noticed a poster for a cricket match organised by Gorey Boat Owners Association 'on the Écreviére Bank'. Thoughts of sunnier days sprang to mind and being a recently retired Wednesday evening player (best figures; opening with a five wicket maiden and 6 for 10 off four overs) I was intrigued. Although I had visited Jersey several times and felt that I was beginning to get to know the place I had not heard of the Écreviére Bank and asked where it was exactly, to which the reply came, 'it's just to the south east of the Écréhous. It's made of shell fragments and only appears on very low spring tides'. And I thought bowling into the sun off a run-up scattered with fresh mole hills and sheep droppings was a handicap.

After about forty minutes Maître Île, the largest of the three islets of the Écréhous was sighted. We headed for a point to the east of the island, our pilotage marks being a large shark's fin of a rock, Bigorne, which has to be kept positioned between two low lying outcrops beyond it. As our destination Marmotiére came into sight a little to the north of Maître Île we changed direction to port. As our guide this time we kept the island's flagpole positioned in front of two vertical black panels mounted on a frame behind it. Apparently getting in here is not as difficult as it looks on the charts. I had to take their word for that.

As we approached Marmotiére individual houses began to emerge from a dark grey silhouette of rock and roofs; a jumble of walls perched precariously on their tiny pile of rock, a street in the sea.

We rounded the west side of the island to approach the States mooring buoy and four more houses came into view, each perched upon its own individual piece of rock, with two of them joined to Marmotiére by an impressive curving bank of shingle. What a remarkable sight. This is what Venice must have looked like a millennium ago just before construction was about to commence, when only the builders' huts had been erected.

One other boat was moored nearby but no one could be seen. After tying up at the buoy we rowed ashore. We had arrived at half tide down and did not expect the sea level to fall dramatically further. At close quarters it became clear that the pale coloured shingle bank was stepped, indicating the heights of the various tides, the level of each step being picked out with a thin straggly line of seaweed. The highest showed that at a particularly high spring tide nearly all of the bank would be submerged and the sea would rise almost to the walls of some of the houses.

Although the largest island of the group is Maître Île, it is on Marmotiére that nearly all the houses are sited. None of them are permanently occupied, being much-prized retreats for the few Jersey families fortunate to own one.

A cluster of about eighteen tiny buildings are huddled together in a tight picturesque group, with several blocks of three or four houses separated by small passageways which all lead into a small sheltered yard where thrift grows in abundance. Many of them are so small they must be a single room, but it was impossible to tell, all were boarded up. Although the few exposed pieces of walling

156

Les Écréhous reef

suggested, quite naturally, that they were built of granite blocks, surprisingly most of the houses had been rendered and some painted. All the properties looked neat, tidy and well cared for.

No one else appeared to be here, we seemed to have the place to ourselves and it was a little eerie as we explored, half expecting someone to appear. A dinghy leaning against a wall and a tiny patch of soil planted with a variety of herbs, sheltered from the wind by roof slates held upright with pebbles, suggested that the lack of occupants was an uncommon occurrence.

I spent some time sketching this idyllic spot. I often try to avoid buildings as they seldom add much to a good natural scene, but in this case it was their very presence which transformed what would

otherwise be a reef of isolated rocks into a rather bizarre version of paradise. While sketching I became aware that, at last, a slow brightening up process had commenced. The dim outline of Gorey Castle and a section of French coastline had begun to emerge from the gloom.

Our reverie was interrupted by the approach of an unusually rigged sailing vessel. This was clearly going to be one of those 'one for the album' moments. You take one of me with it in the background, then I'll take one of you. Their line of approach suggested that they were not merely passing close by but intended to heave to in a sheltered spot and drop anchor.

The appearance of their Tricolour did not actually set sirens wailing and warning lights flashing, but it had the same effect nevertheless. What a transformation!

Union Jack time

One moment we were metaphorically lounging in deck chairs in our fleece lined leather flying jackets, sipping tea from willow patterned china cups and munching cucumber sandwiches with the crusts removed, the next, Tally-ho, chocks were away and Spitfires were taking to the air. Wait a moment, I thought they were on our side? You must be joking. This was a red, white and blue striped rag to a bull, and the bull had his head down and was repeatedly dragging a hoof across the ground.

Where did those people appear from? We were not alone after all, one of the isolated houses at the opposite end of the shingle bank had been occupied all along and suddenly the only thing that mattered was to get the Union Jack up the flagpole to remind those French interlopers whose island this was.

Ownership of the Écréhous and the Minkies has long been a point of dispute between Britain – in support of Jersey – and France. The French claimed that Les Écréhous were given to them in 1203, the year before King John lost the Duchy of Normandy to France. They were in fact given to a Norman monastery on the understanding that a light be built for ships and a chapel for souls. The ruins of a priory can still be seen on Maître Île, but no light was ever built. The case finally went to the International Court of Justice in the Hague in 1953. Legal argument went on for several weeks, requiring 26 public sessions where documents going back to mediaeval times were considered. The final judgement took more than an hour to deliver and awarded sovereignty to Britain, with the Écréhous becoming part of the Jersey parish of St Martin.

We walked away from the houses along the shingle to get a better view. Sails were being furled, it looked like they intended to stay for a while. The boat was a bisquine, a traditional three masted lugger about 18 metres long and, despite being French, it looked very impressive. I was a little disappointed to discover later that it was a modern replica, built, however, in the traditional way on the beach at Cancalaise.

As the crew prepared to come ashore, we prepared to depart. I had enjoyed my time here, it was quite magical in fact, but now that other people were about, some of the magic had gone. I am sure that a good time to return would be when most of the part-time residents are here enjoying the various delights of the sea. Until then, we left them to deal with the small matter of international relations.